NEW DIRECTIONS FOR COMMUNITY COLLEGES

Arthur M. Cohen
EDITOR-IN-CHIEF

Florence B. Brawer
ASSOCIATE EDITOR

Graduate and Continuing Education for Community College Leaders: What It Means Today

James C. Palmer
Illinois State University, Normal

Stephen G. Katsinas
University of Toledo

EDITORS

Number 95, Fall 1996

JOSSEY-BASS PUBLISHERS
San Francisco

Clearinghouse for Community Colleges

GRADUATE AND CONTINUING EDUCATION FOR COMMUNITY COLLEGE
LEADERS: WHAT IT MEANS TODAY
James C. Palmer, Stephen G. Katsinas (eds.)
New Directions for Community Colleges, no. 95
Volume XXIV, number 3
Arthur M. Cohen, Editor-in-Chief
Florence B. Brawer, Associate Editor

Microfilm copies of issues and articles are available in 16mm and 35mm,
as well as microfiche in 105mm, through University Microfilms Inc.,
300 North Zeeb Road, Ann Arbor, Michigan 48106-1346.

ISSN 0194-3081   ISBN 0-7879-9892-3

NEW DIRECTIONS FOR COMMUNITY COLLEGES is part of The Jossey-Bass
Higher and Adult Education Series and is published quarterly by Jossey-
Bass Inc., Publishers, 350 Sansome Street, San Francisco, California
94104-1342 in association with the ERIC Clearinghouse for Community
Colleges. Periodicals postage paid at San Francisco, California, and at
additional mailing offices. POSTMASTER: Send address changes to New
Directions for Community Colleges, Jossey-Bass Inc., Publishers, 350
Sansome Street, San Francisco, California 94104-1342.

SUBSCRIPTIONS for 1996 cost $53.00 for individuals and $89.00 for institutions, agencies, and libraries.

THE MATERIAL in this publication is based on work sponsored wholly or
in part by the Office of Educational Research and Improvement, U.S.
Department of Education, under contract number RI-93-00-2003. Its con-
tents do not necessarily reflect the views of the Department, or any other
agency of the U.S. Government.

EDITORIAL CORRESPONDENCE should be sent to the Editor-in-Chief, Arthur
M. Cohen, at the ERIC Clearinghouse for Community Colleges, Univer-
sity of California, 3051 Moore Hall, 405 Hilgard Avenue, Los Angeles,
California 90095-1521.

Cover photograph © Rene Sheret, After Image, Los Angeles, California,
1990.

Manufactured in the United States of America on Lyons Falls
Pathfinder Tradebook. This paper is acid-free and 100 percent
totally chlorine-free.

CONTENTS

EDITORS' NOTES

Graduate study of the community college constitutes a small but well-established academic specialty. Its rise in the three decades following World War II paralleled the rapid establishment of community colleges during those years, testifying to the modern university's stake in graduate education for the ever expanding and ever more specialized professions. The professors working within this specialty, never more than a hundred at any one time (Cohen, Palmer, and Zwemer, 1986), are sometimes members of university departments devoted solely to community college leadership. Programs at the University of Texas, Austin, and at North Carolina State University are examples. More often, however, these professors work as community college specialists within academic departments that offer doctoral study for individuals pursuing careers at a variety of levels of the educational enterprise, including community colleges.

The urgent need to fill administrative slots at a growing number of community colleges has subsided in the past two decades, bringing to the fore fundamental questions about the intellectual purpose and academic integrity of graduate preparation programs for community college leaders. Program establishment and growth are no longer their own justification, and commentators have called for a reexamination of graduate curricula focusing on community college education. For example, Fryer (1984) argued that graduate preparation programs often do not foster the administrative and interpersonal competencies needed by community college administrators. Richardson (1987) offered a blunter critique, suggesting that some university programs for community college leaders might need to be shut down. Highlighting the lack of agreement about what attainment of a doctorate in community college education actually means, he warned, "To the extent that a doctoral degree in community college leadership is viewed as a 'union card' or certificate of attendance, those who hold it run the risk of being perceived as the product of an inferior graduate program." He called for the specification of "conditions of excellence in graduate education for community college leaders," arguing that programs conforming to those conditions should be supported while those that do not "should be encouraged to improve or go out of business" (p. 41).

It is within this context that the chapters in this volume provide critical perspectives on the current status of community college education as an academic specialty. In Chapter One, Raymond J. Young takes a historical view, describing the events that coincided with the development of community college leadership programs in the immediate post–World War II era and speculating on the legacy of those formative years. Stephen G. Katsinas follows in Chapter Two with a discussion of the challenges faced by professors in describing and studying the diverse types of community colleges, suggesting that professors and practitioners alike have all too often depicted two-year colleges as a homogeneous set of institutions.

In Chapter Three, George B. Vaughan and Barbara Scott turn to the ways that graduate professors might hone student writing skills, arguing that attention to writing is often missing in debates about what constitutes an effective graduate program for educational leaders. Chapter Four, by Joseph N. Hankin, and Chapter Five, by Berta Vigil Laden, consider the continuing education needs of community college leaders and the professional development programs that meet those needs. Their work underscores the important ways that ongoing professional development efforts complement graduate study in educational administration.

The next two chapters consider the potential influence of graduate education on the nature of community college leadership itself. In Chapter Six, Barbara K. Townsend examines the gatekeeping role played by graduate preparation programs, arguing that university professors can do more to bring women and minorities into the leadership ranks of community colleges. Barbara S. Gibson-Benninger, James L. Ratcliff, and Robert A. Rhoads follow in Chapter Seven with a discussion that also stresses the inclusion of diverse populations; the authors maintain that graduate programs should help college leaders understand and apply principles of democratic administration that value wide-ranging participation in decision making.

Professorial obligations to community college practitioners are then considered in Chapter Eight, by George A. Baker III, and Chapter Nine, by James C. Palmer. Baker examines the role of the professor as a coleader and motivator within the community college movement. Palmer takes a different stance, viewing the professor as an outside critic whose scholarly roles sometimes conflict with the practitioner's role as institutional advocate.

Chapter Ten, by James C. Palmer and Stephen G. Katsinas, concludes the volume with a review of previous literature on graduate education for community college leaders, focusing especially on the aims of graduate programming and the difficulties that sometimes emerge in professor-practitioner relations. The review links previous literature to the themes discussed in the chapters. Attention is paid to the literature on the graduate education of community college leaders and not to the wider literature on graduate study in higher education generally.

Most of these chapters were developed from papers delivered at the spring 1995 meeting of the Council of Universities and Colleges (CUC). The meeting was devoted to dialogue about the status of the academic specialty that CUC members, mostly university faculty, engage in. The vitality and utility of this specialty will depend on a continued debate about intellectual purpose and professorial roles. This is especially important as the conditions that gave rise to this specialty in the immediate post-war era—institutional growth and a concomitant demand for new administrators—give way to the present-day challenges faced by contemporary community college administrators, whose institutions are now a long-established part of the educational status quo.

References

Cohen, A. M., Palmer, J. C., and Zwemer, K. D. *Key Resources on Community Colleges.* San Francisco: Jossey-Bass, 1986.

Fryer, T. W., Jr. "Developing Leaders Through Graduate Education." In R. L. Alfred, P. A. Elsner, R. J. LeCroy, and N. Armes (eds.), *Emerging Roles for Community College Leaders.* New Directions for Community Colleges, no. 46. San Francisco: Jossey-Bass, 1984.

Richardson, R. C., Jr. "A Question of Quality: University Programs for Community College Leaders." *Community, Technical, and Junior College Journal,* 1987, 57 (4), 39–41.

JAMES C. PALMER *is associate professor of educational administration and foundations at Illinois State University, Normal, Illinois.*

STEPHEN G. KATSINAS *is associate professor of higher education at the University of Toledo, Toledo, Ohio.*

*This chapter discusses the interplay between developments in the field
and the emergence of graduate and continuing education programs for
community college leaders in the thirty years following World War II.
It concludes with a critical analysis of the legacy of those programs.*

Legacy of the Post-WWII Growth Years for Community College Leadership Programs

Raymond J. Young

In the first three decades following World War II, a primary focus of public
education policymakers was the proper establishment of publicly controlled
community colleges. It was in this era of rapid institutional growth and atten-
dant uncertainty that university-based graduate programs for community college leaders emerged, taking the form with which we are familiar today. This
chapter provides an overview of the key factors and circumstances that led to
the development of these programs. The intent is to provide the reader with a
sense of the interplay between developments in the field and the initial development and emergence of graduate and continuing education programs for
community college leaders. The chapter covers events from 1945 through
1975 and concludes with an interpretive analysis of the legacy of those years,
focusing especially on the impact of philanthropic foundations (such as the W.
K. Kellogg Foundation) that supported the development of graduate programs
in community college leadership.

The Early Post-WWII Years to 1960

Up until the mid-1950s, the development of public two-year colleges had been
erratic, haphazard, and largely without plan. College establishment was subject to the special economic and altruistic motives of local communities, the
political whims of legislators, and the missionary work of a few public university personnel. Most of the new colleges were upward extensions of high
schools and some, particularly in California, Texas, and Mississippi, were

established in areas that contained two or more school districts maintaining high schools.

Legislators in a few states had foreseen the possibility that too many financially and educationally inefficient two-year colleges might be established if local community aspirations guided the burgeoning two-year college movement. But with the exception of California, local colleges were established in the absence of an overall plan for higher education or two-year college development. Efforts to guide college planning in systematic ways were just beginning. The first full-scale comprehensive citizens' participatory study for the establishment of a public two-year college was organized and conducted in the Illinois Wood River–Alton area (Young, 1957). Criteria for founding public two-year colleges developed by Fretwell (1954) were operationalized in the study, and research was conducted to determine whether the criteria were met. Other such studies soon followed in the Canton, Freeport, and Kewanee areas of Illinois. Such grassroots citizen involvement was seen as a prerequisite to persuade voters of the need for a two-year college, if conditions were favorable.

In mid-decade, demographic projections portended the higher education enrollment explosion of the 1960s. Fearing a topsy-turvy, unmanaged explosion of two-year college development, state-level educational agencies were urged to take responsibility for orderly college development based on empirically determined community needs (Young, 1959). Taking a cue from the pacesetting studies in California, which led to that state's master plan, other states such as Illinois, Michigan, and Florida developed higher education master plans that included public two-year colleges.

The need for rational planning was underscored by the fact that of the existing public two-year colleges in the Midwest, only about 30 percent were regionally accredited in the mid-1950s. An initial workshop was conducted at the 1957 annual meeting of the North Central Association of Colleges and Schools for junior college administrators and trustees of nonaccredited two-year colleges. By 1960, these workshop sessions had grown from a few participants meeting for a two-hour session in a small conference room to half-day sessions in a hall designed to seat over a hundred persons. By the early 1960s, regional accreditation was to become an essential condition for institutional certification by various state and federal agencies, and a prerequisite of philanthropic foundations for honoring grant proposals.

University professors of higher education became involved in these planning efforts. By 1957, there were at least half a dozen university-based professors who were being called upon constantly to assist local community organizations in establishing two-year colleges. In that year, this group of professors began to meet at the American Association of Junior Colleges annual conference. These meetings eventually led to the creation of the Council of Universities and Colleges, the American Association of Community Colleges' affiliated council of professors of higher education who specialize in community college–related research.

Continuing in the tradition of Koos and Eells, who were the first prominent university professors to devote their scholarship to the community colleges, university professors also offered scholarly perspectives on the community college movement. The close of the 1950s saw the first nationwide study of two-year colleges conducted using normative survey research methods (Medsker, 1960). Several university-based faculty contributed data to this study on the performance of transfer students. The overall findings corroborated the fact that, after an initial decline in performance (the so-called *transfer shock* phenomenon), the transfer students performed as well as students who had begun their university work as freshmen in that university. In years ahead, this finding was significant in helping convince residents in local communities a two-year college could offer two years of quality collegiate education as well as a whole range of occupationally related college-credit work demanded increasingly by government, business, and industry and not being provided by existing four-year colleges.

The end of the 1950s also saw the publication of a general book on the two-year college (Thornton, 1960), which would be widely used as a required text in graduate classes for community college leaders. This was the first major text about two-year colleges in many decades, save one book by the executive secretary of the American Association of Junior Colleges (Bogue, 1950). As editor of the Thornton manuscript for the publishers, this writer suggested the title should be *The Community Junior College,* helping readers to bridge the gap between the traditional concept of the junior college and the evolving concept of the community college. The suggested title was accepted, and, in retrospect, served the intended purpose of helping people link the institution with the notion of community and all that this term suggests in terms of a broadened scope of function and service. The Thornton book was subsequently reissued in second and third editions and served as a standard text on the subject until the mid-1970s.

The period from 1945 to 1960 was a transitional period, the launching pad prior to the great expansion of public community colleges in the United States. University professors specializing in higher education were often driven by the need to help society plan for and understand the new community college systems that were emerging. They also helped educate a new generation of administrators who would be specially trained in the leadership of these new institutions, replacing the older generation of college leaders who had often started their careers in school systems or in the university setting.

From 1960 to the Mid-1970s

By the early 1960s, it was clear that a significant enlargement of the higher education enterprise would soon occur. The pace of public two-year college establishment seemed to increase all at once, at both the institutional and state levels. Between the mid-1960s and 1975, new colleges were being developed at the rate of one a week for a time. Any hope that the state could require a pre-establishment study of local need for a college went out the window. Some universities, particularly in Ohio and Pennsylvania, had begun developing branches to accommodate bulging main campus enrollments. Except in a few states that had some semblance of a plan or some general legislative enactment in place for the orderly development of public two-year colleges, it was fortunate that much of the development was in the larger cities. Many of them had one or more other institutions of higher education. In most metropolitan areas, campus master plans were developed, just as there had been an overall plan developed early in Chicago for establishing new City College campuses.

Two-year college leaders and state agency personnel began to discern merit in patterns of two-year college district organization patterned after those in California, Texas, and Mississippi, which enabled the colleges to be separated from the public school districts and organized in a district created just for that purpose. Because of increasing costs and enrollments in public school districts, school district authorities were generally happy to support the notion of college separation. At the state level, various arrangements were being made to provide some form of oversight of the two-year college development. In some states, such as Illinois, a billet was created in the office of the State Superintendent of Schools. Other states created coordinating boards for the purpose. Over time, most of the original arrangements evolved into forms of state coordinating boards or councils. By the end of the 1960s, it became clear that greater focus was needed to promote effective planning for community college education on a statewide basis.

Due to the complexities of increased size and broadened functions of higher education to accommodate an increasing heterogeneous enrollment (especially at the free-standing public two-year colleges), the demand for administrative leadership was about to transcend the ability of the system to generate new leaders. The emerging public two-year colleges required of administrators a mentality and set of skills different than those of either public school or university administrators. These developments and trends had not gone unnoticed by a few existing senior colleges and universities, nor by the foundations. To assist in coping with the problems of leadership supply, some universities began offering graduate programs to prepare persons to work in leadership positions in the two-year colleges. The number of universities and colleges offering professional graduate work in higher education expanded from twenty-seven in 1945 to eighty-seven in the 1962–63 year (Ewing and Stickler, 1964).

While a course in the junior college was included in the original higher education curriculum proposed by G. Stanley Hall, only a few institutions offered graduate work in higher education prior to 1945. These included Ohio State University, Teachers College of Columbia University, the University of Chicago, the University of Pittsburgh, the University of California at Berkeley, and the University of Michigan (Goodchild, 1991). By 1960, major centers or institutes for the study of higher education had been established at Teachers College of Columbia University, the University of California at Berkeley, and the University of Michigan. In 1962, planning to establish centers had begun in six other universities, and operations were beginning in three more. Two or three additional universities had plans to establish centers in the near future (Ewing and Stickler, 1964).

Philanthropic foundations were to play a major role in the expansion of higher education programs that housed specializations in community college education, as well as in the few free-standing community college leadership programs. In fact, foundations have had a great impact on our understanding of community colleges since the 1920s, when the Commonwealth Foundation funded the first study of junior colleges (Koos, 1924). It is not the intent of this chapter to inclusively mention or slight any of the many foundations that have generously assisted the educational system. It is important, however, to note that the funding priorities of a given foundation often reflected the priorities of personnel then at the helm as well as the objectives for which the foundation had been created.

In the mid-1950s, The Carnegie Foundation recognized the need to prepare and upgrade the skills of administrators for the rapidly expanding colleges and universities in general. It is possible that early Carnegie Foundation grants to a few selected universities stimulated interest among personnel in other foundations to assist with leadership development programming for the fastest-growing component of the post-secondary system, the community colleges. Using community colleges to extend access to postsecondary education for adults would later become a long-term agenda item for Kellogg, Ford, and other philanthropic foundations.

In the 1958–59 year, representatives of the University of Michigan (Jesse Bogue and Algo Henderson) and the University of Texas (James Reynolds and C. C. Colvert) held several conferences with officials of the W. K. Kellogg Foundation. They discussed the paucity of graduate programs designed to produce leaders for the emerging two-year colleges and the shortage that would occur in the near future. Later, other university representatives made similar contacts when word got out about possibilities for funding assistance. Reynolds had been heavily involved and associated with the successful University of Texas Kellogg-funded center for the improvement of school district administration during the early 1950s, which in many ways served as a model for Kellogg's later activity in support of community college leadership development. The record of effectiveness of the Texas center, along with the records of some of the twenty-two other funded centers, inspired confidence in the ability of philanthropic assistance to foster improvement in educational leadership.

Kellogg Foundation program officers and the Kellogg board supported varied university approaches to the development of leadership programs. Some universities had community college leadership subsumed within larger departments or programs in higher education; others had self-contained community college leadership programs. Grants were made to ten universities located in California, Florida, Michigan, New York, and Texas. Almost a decade later, grants were made to the Universities of Colorado and Washington. All these grants provided legitimacy to graduate programs in higher education and community college leadership, a point that cannot be overstated, given the traditional emphasis of colleges of education on elementary and secondary education.

Each institution developed highly individualized leadership programs. Some used their grant monies for fellowships; others used the funds to employ additional faculty. Content ranged from heavy emphasis on graduate-level work in the social and behavioral sciences as a substantial part of the doctoral degree to programs limited entirely to courses in education. Most included an internship requirement. Some emphasized the socialization aspect by using a cohort method of progress toward degree completion.

As the author of the University of Michigan proposal, and as a participant in subsequent conferences with Kellogg Foundation personnel, this writer formed several distinct impressions regarding funding of graduate programs for community college leaders. First, the Kellogg Foundation officials, based upon the far-reaching and successful impact their investments had made in improving K–12 school leadership through preservice preparation and in-service programs, were genuinely interested in helping the nation cope with the provision of quality two-year college leadership at universities, in state agencies, and in the community colleges themselves.

Second, it seemed the foundation was interested in institutional initiative and possessed the imagination to experiment with diverse programmatic approaches and in the sharing of information among program directors. Program directors and staff of funded institutes, centers, or programs held periodic meetings each year for this purpose.

Third, the foundation never appeared to expect that the funded programs would begin to supply the demand for administrators. Rather, the programs collectively could serve a leadership role in testing various formats, configurations, and approaches useful to universities throughout the nation that had become sensitized to the need for developing leaders for the two-year colleges.

Fourth, it seemed that the foundation officials were interested in testing whether forms of interinstitutional cooperation and collaboration among universities in programmatic planning could work and endure. The former was largely voluntary, and the latter was mandatory with funding as the incentive.

Fifth, because the University Council for Educational Administration had emerged as a continuing force for fostering leadership improvement in school district administration, it was the expectation that something similar might emerge to carry on improvement efforts in two-year college administration after the grant period concluded. This impression was precipitated by references in early conferences with foundation officials while discussing possibilities for funding assistance for two-year college leadership programs.

Finally, there was an overriding expectation that, for the long term, graduate-level community college leadership programs that were made possible, or enhanced by, external funding assistance would become institutionalized as an integral part of the operation, with adequate internal resources phased in to ensure continued existence. Time has demonstrated that this objective was only partially achieved.

Current Needs and Demands

In 1995, the American Association of Community and Junior Colleges reported that well over eleven hundred two-year colleges were members (p. 5). Although not all two-year colleges hold membership in the association, most do. Some metropolitan public two-year college systems consider all their campuses to be integral parts of a single college, while in other instances each campus in the system is considered an autonomous college in its own right, held together with others by a loose, district-level coordinating federation. The point to be made here is that the number of functioning campuses is probably closer to twelve hundred—about double the number that existed in 1950. The size and complexity of public institutions have increased manyfold, requiring administrative staffs of considerable size. Added to the demand for qualified institutional administrators is the demand in each of fifty states for personnel to staff the offices of state-level directors and state-level coordinating boards, councils, or offices. Additionally, there is demand created by colleges and universities for personnel to staff professorial positions to teach in the leadership programs.

At the end of the 1960s, in contrast to earlier times, most institutional governing boards had come to insist on the doctorate as the minimum educational criterion for individuals seeking administrative positions in two-year colleges. By the mid-1970s, the transition had been virtually completed as the older administrators retired, were replaced, or left for some other reason. Men and women who assumed major administrative positions in most of the newly established two-year colleges, state offices, and four-year colleges and universities in the late 1960s and 1970s have already begun to retire in large numbers. Today, one can count on a few fingers of one hand the number of presidents still at the helm of the college they helped establish. As the country lunges forward into the twenty-first century, based on demographics alone (to say nothing of significant socioeconomic factors at work), the demand for well-qualified two-year college administrators will continue to increase, but the increase will probably be at a more steady pace, somewhat slower than in the post-war era.

The Legacy Critique

The two-year college leadership programs of the 1960s, financially assisted by Kellogg Foundation grants in a few selected universities, produced most of the authorities and leaders in the field today, as well as many of the practicing chief administrators. These programs' existence sensitized personnel in colleges and universities throughout the nation to the demand for personnel with graduate degrees to work in two-year colleges. Goodchild and Fife (1991) estimate that over a hundred such programs exist across the nation. Perhaps the time has come to consider whether it would be desirable to concentrate leadership programs in the graduate schools of far fewer colleges and universities, rather than to encourage the existence of so many graduate programs with small enrollments and staff lacking breadth or depth—lacking critical mass, so to speak.

Should there be some form of specialized accreditation to control the apparent proliferation of such programs, or will they just fade away due to retirements and economic pressures?

External funding for some leadership centers enabled them to develop strong staffs, and opened the way for them to attract additional funding from a variety of other sources on a continuing basis for further program development. The influence of these centers has been profound. Some centers were able to engage the interest of professors from the social and behavioral sciences, as well as other disciplines, and involve them in the leadership programs and research related to the field. It is from those institutions truly meaningful and significant research has come. As university graduate programs came to perform a credentialing function (Goodchild and Fife, 1991), doctoral and faculty research appears to have degenerated almost exclusively into picture taking through normative methodologies. Synthesis, evaluation, and analysis, to say nothing of relational and cause-and-effect inquiries, have been sparse or nonexistent. While there is a proper place for these normative kinds of study couched in some kind of theoretical framework, there is danger that the field is resorting to mere navel gazing and examining tracks in the sand.

One can wonder who is furthering the cutting edge, and if the efforts to meet the credentialing demand will ultimately lead to a complete stalemate of knowledge in the field of two-year college education. No nationally recognized center for theoretically oriented community college basic research emerged from the foundation-sponsored centers, as had been the case as a result of the 1950s funding of centers to improve elementary and secondary school administration. Perhaps too much attention was given in graduate programs to praxis and the mechanics of administration, rather than to the whys behind the hows of two-year college administration, and to the institution's nature and role in the broader context of education in a democratic society.

Although the Council of Universities and Colleges (CUC) had its beginning several years prior to the existence of Kellogg grants to assist in leadership program development, the sudden increase in numbers of people associated with those programs in the early 1960s helped give permanence and viability to the organization. The council was originally conceived as a forum by which professors of two-year college education could share and exchange information and experiences about graduate programs. While the directors of leadership programs, and sometimes other new staff of the funded centers, had their own meetings for this purpose, nearly all participated also in annual meetings of CUC, where information became available to a broader college and university clientele. Unlike the University Council on Educational Administration, the CUC did not include, to the same extent, both practicing administrators and professors. With inputs from the leadership program participants, the CUC has accomplished well the purposes for which it was created, and in addition has encouraged and recognized research and scholarly activities of its members, and of doctoral studies supervised by members.

What seems lacking in terms of legacy are valid, thorough evaluations of the funded leadership programs. To conduct such an evaluation, one would have to establish what the long-range goals and expectations were for funding such programs in the first place. Was it a purpose to produce enough administrators to fill administrative vacancies of the rapidly expanding numbers of new two-year colleges and of retiring older personnel? To test the effectiveness of different approaches for preparing administrative personnel? To produce leaders who would occupy positions of broad influence in state-level administrative and coordinating positions? To produce leaders who would occupy positions as university professors and develop other university programs to prepare greater numbers of administrators? To improve the volume of information disseminated regarding administrative issues, concerns, and problems? To test the effectiveness of multi-university cooperative efforts versus single university efforts? To stimulate the development of administrator preparation programs in various other universities by highlighting the need through the funding of a few selected major universities? To improve the performance of new trustees and of administrators already in the field? Did the purposes include all of these and perhaps others not mentioned? Clearly, such an assessment would be a daunting task. How well such purposes might have been accomplished remains unanswered. What is known, however, is that evaluation of individual university programs was not to be a part of the funded grant proposals during that era; that responsibility was left to each individual university as part of its ongoing procedures.

In view of today's needs, the challenge of providing administrative leadership for two-year colleges exists in a vastly different social milieu than that of the 1950s, 1960s, and early 1970s. Several points deserve careful consideration. First, the types of persons and the skills required to maintain and improve upon a system may be somewhat different from those required to initiate the establishment and development of new institutions. Educational programs designed to prepare leaders for today and tomorrow should take account of this change as well as all the advancements in communication systems and available technology. Second—and this has become crystal clear and self-evident to persons who experienced the adolescent period of two-year college development—the task of preparing administrative leadership cannot be accomplished once and for all with a one-shot infusion of funds and attention. It may be time for a thorough assessment of manpower supply and demand and of the attributes needed by effective two-year college leaders. It may also be time for the development of a center for theoretical basic research on community colleges. Probably the greatest legacy of the past is that there are multiple approaches to these tasks, and that the job can be accomplished. Developments in the field need to be reflected in university-based graduate and continuing education programs for community college leaders.

References

American Association of Community and Junior Colleges. *The 1995–96 AACC Annual.* Washington, D.C.: American Association of Community Junior Colleges, 1995.

Bogue, J. P. *The Community College.* New York: McGraw-Hill, 1950.

Ewing, J. C., and Stickler, W. H. "Progress in the Development of Higher Education as a Field of Professional Graduate Study and Research." *Journal of Teacher Education,* 1964, *15,* 397–403.

Fretwell, E. K., Jr. *Founding Public Junior Colleges*. New York: Teachers College, Columbia University, 1954.

Goodchild, L. F. "Higher Education as a Field of Study: Its Origins, Programs, and Purposes, 1893–1960." In J. D. Fife and L. F. Goodchild (eds.), *Administration as a Profession*. New Directions for Higher Education, no. 76. San Francisco: Jossey-Bass, 1991.

Goodchild, L. F., and Fife, J. D. "Conclusion." In J. D. Fife and L. F. Goodchild (eds.), *Administration as a Profession*. New Directions for Higher Education, no. 76. San Francisco: Jossey-Bass, 1991.

Koos, L. V. *The Junior College*. Minneapolis: University of Minnesota Press, 1924.

Medsker, L. *The Junior College: Progress and Prospect*. New York: McGraw-Hill, 1960.

Thornton, J. W., Jr. *The Community Junior College*. New York: Wiley, 1960.

Young, R. J. *Citizens Survey of Community College Possibilities: A Survey of the East Alton–Wood River, Illinois, High School District*. Urbana: Office of Field Services, College of Education, University of Illinois, 1957.

Young, R. J. "Survey of Junior College Possibilities: A State Responsibility." *Junior College Journal*, 1959, 29, 245–253.

RAYMOND J. YOUNG is professor emeritus, Washington State University. He served as director of the Community College Leadership Institute at the University of Michigan in the late 1950s and early 1960s.

*This chapter argues that a major gap in our understanding
of community colleges is the need to recognize the diversity of
institutional settings. A Carnegie-style classification system for
community colleges is proposed, with a discussion of implications
for graduate programs preparing community college leaders.*

Preparing Leaders for Diverse Institutional Settings

Stephen G. Katsinas

Implicit in much of the higher education literature is the notion that great
homogeneity exists among and between community colleges in the United
States. While they share a commitment to open access, comprehensiveness, and
responsiveness to local needs, community colleges are in fact a diverse group
of institutions. This diversity is reflected in geography, demography, governance, and institutional size. All affect college culture and the roles played by
community college educators and leaders who complete graduate programs in
higher education. What works in a large, multicampus urban community college system does not necessarily work in a small, rural setting, and vice versa.

These differences are well known by experienced community college leaders and by the boards of trustees they serve (Katsinas, 1993). Regional geo-
graphic and demographic traits are reported by the institutions themselves in
virtually every executive position description found in *Community College
Times, Community College Week,* or the *Chronicle of Higher Education.* The intent
is to attract applicants who can function in the college's unique circumstances.
Successful candidates for these positions are aware of the vast differences in
management knowledge and personal leadership style required to administer
a single-campus rural community college as opposed to a five-campus urban
metropolitan district.

Unfortunately, these differences have not been adequately recognized in
the community college literature. The general tendency to treat community
colleges as homogeneous institutions prevails, particularly for research university economists and sociologists who are not themselves directly engaged
in graduate and professional education programs for community college leaders. Breneman and Nelson's influential book *Financing Community Colleges*

(1981) offers a prime example in its advocacy of high-tuition, high–financial aid policies. Their underlying assumption was that the widespread availability of federal student financial aid removed the need for states to keep tuition low or nonexistent at their publicly controlled community colleges to promote access. Nowhere in their analysis, however, did they account for the fact that students in different regions have different nontuition costs associated with college attendance. Most students in urban areas, for example, can easily access publicly subsidized mass transit. Students in the eleven rural community colleges interviewed as part of a Ford Foundation–sponsored research project in the fall of 1995 said that access to a reliable automobile was an absolute prerequisite to college attendance. Focus groups with students attending rural community colleges in Massachusetts and Minnesota, states with tuition in excess of $1,900 per year, revealed that the total cost of college attendance was well beyond the maximum available federal Pell grant of $2,350 per year. Results of the Ford Foundation research project, to be published elsewhere, revealed that many students who started college on a full-time basis dropped out or reverted to part-time status in their second year of study.

Those engaged in graduate and continuing education programs to prepare community college leaders clearly need to conduct their work in ways that recognize such institutional differences. A major impediment to this goal is the lack of a recognized typology that distributes two-year colleges according to institutional settings, providing a nomenclature for what the field implicitly recognizes as generally accepted differences. This chapter examines the practical value of a typology to the study of higher education, suggests a community college classification scheme, and examines implications for graduate programs that prepare community college leaders.

Why an Institutional Typology?

The importance of an institutional typology is readily apparent in the Carnegie Classification System of Institutions of Higher Education, which frames much of what is known about American higher education. Originally released in 1973, and refined and updated in 1976, 1987, and 1994, the Carnegie classification system divides four-year colleges into subcategories based on levels and numbers of degrees offered (doctoral, master's, baccalaureate, and associate), selectivity in the admissions process, and the volume of federal research dollars received. There are eight separate and distinct subcategories for four-year institutions within the Carnegie classifications. As a result, reliable information on the varied types of four-year colleges is readily available. Researchers scanning the Dissertation Abstracts International (DAI) data base can confidently use the Carnegie nomenclature to find theses that relate directly to "research universities" as opposed to "liberal arts colleges." For example, as of January 2, 1996, 3,564 DAI entries related to the former and 829 entries related to the latter.

Unfortunately, the same cannot be said for community colleges. The Carnegie classification system places two-year institutions into a single, one-size-fits-all grouping. Of the 4,331 DAI entries retrievable using the term "community colleges" as of January 2, 1996, 177, or about 4 percent, were listed under "rural community colleges"; 56, or about 1.3 percent, under "suburban community colleges"; and 211, or about 5 percent, under "urban community colleges." Another 23 dissertations were listed under "Tribal Colleges," 23 under "private junior colleges," and 40 under "proprietary colleges." Unfortunately, because no commonly understood nomenclature exists, these terms reflect the subjective understandings of the dissertation authors as opposed to objective distinctions, and generalizations from this body of work are limited.

The lack of an agreed-upon typology has significant implications for our understanding of community colleges because, like knowledge in most social science fields, additions to the higher education knowledge base are made incrementally. Each doctoral dissertation study using the specific Carnegie subgroupings adds to what is already known about those institutions. The most recent Carnegie classification system (1994) included for the first time the category of Tribal Colleges, thereby spurring new research interest in these institutions.

The lack of an agreed-upon typology also unintentionally creates a wedge between university professors and their students engaged in community college–related research, and practitioners in the field. For example, absent a typology, students writing dissertations on community colleges often rely on surveys of the entire population of community colleges, because no basis exists upon which to choose a stratified sample. Inasmuch as some of the most valuable research is found in dissertations, this problem is not insignificant. A national survey of 1,200 community colleges using the American Association of Community Colleges mailing list can cost a student in excess of $1,500. At the institutional level, it is not uncommon for community college CEOs to receive between four and seven detailed national surveys each week, each of which takes twenty to thirty minutes to fill out. Given time pressures, many choose not to respond. The lack of an agreed-upon classification system for community colleges also makes it difficult for researchers outside doctoral programs in higher and community college education to benefit from the expertise and understanding of experienced researchers in the field, reinforcing the notion of homogeneity among two-year institutions. An agreed-upon classification system would help students and researchers in and out of the field to develop stratified samples that would reduce financial costs associated with research while lowering the overall burden of filling out surveys. The result would be a simultaneous increase in the generalizability of research.

In a personal communication with the author in January 1993, Clark Kerr indicated that although the development of a classification system for community colleges would improve the precision of research, this task was beyond the expertise of the Carnegie research staff in the 1960s and early 1970s. But the need for a more detailed typology still exists. As Kempner (1993) stated at an American Association of Community Colleges Symposium Session in 1993, "We need an architecture that recognizes the diversity of these institutions."

Kempner noted that the failure to develop an appropriate classification system damaged community colleges, in that public policy researchers typically assume all community colleges are exactly alike in terms of state-assigned missions, functions, organizational resources, and complexity.

How should a community college taxonomy be constructed? Table 2.1 shows a proposed classification system that could be folded into the existing Carnegie system. Developed using objective data from the U.S. Department of Commerce, the Bureau of the Census (1990, 1991), and the U.S. Department of Education's National Center for Education Statistics' Integrated Postsecondary Education Data System (IPEDS) (1994), this classification scheme is the result of nearly four years of work, with the support of the Ford Foundation. This work has benefitted from the contributions of Milam (1995), whose doctoral dissertation tested the validity of the categories within the public community college sector using 1990 IPEDS data, and Vincent A. Lacey of Southern Illinois University, who assisted with analyzing the 1993 IPEDS data shown in the table.

Proposed are three major categories of two-year colleges: publicly controlled colleges (1,074), privately controlled colleges (1,497), and federally chartered and special use institutions (229). The 1,074 publicly controlled institutions are

Table 2.1. A Classification System for Community Colleges

	Number of Institutions	Number of Students Served
PUBLICLY CONTROLLED TWO-YEAR INSTITUTIONS	1,070	5,509,280
Rural community colleges	736	1,773,066
Small (<1,000 students)	216	116,124
Medium-sized (1,000–2,499)	245	426,191
Large (2,500+)	275	1,230,751
Suburban community colleges	211	1,920,034
Single campus	171	1,196,073
Multicampus	40	723,961
Urban community colleges	123	1,816,180
Single campus	65	417,744
Multicampus	58	1,398,436
PRIVATELY CONTROLLED TWO-YEAR INSTITUTIONS	836	338,195
Private, nonprofit	116	73,179
Proprietary	720	265,016
FEDERALLY CHARTERED AND SPECIAL USE INSTITUTIONS	595	133,544
Tribal Colleges	29	13,938
Special use institutions	566	119,606
TOTAL	2,501	5,981,019

Source: Institutions classified by the author using data from the 1990 Census and the 1993 IPEDS surveys. Student enrollment data represent preliminary analysis of 1993 IPEDS by the author.

further subdivided into the categories of rural community colleges (766), suburban community colleges (205), and urban community colleges (103).

Gaps in the Literature

These proposed classifications of community colleges have practical implications for the graduate and continuing education of community college leaders, offering a framework to understand the diverse environments in which these leaders work. Table 2.2, "Testable Hypotheses Regarding Diversity Among Public Community Colleges," is drawn from work over the past four years with the IPEDS data, Milam's analysis of the 1990 IPEDS, and observations from visits to over 130 community colleges in thirty-two states over a ten-year period. Table 2.2 also draws upon the author's experience as an employee of Miami-Dade Community College, one of the nation's largest multicampus urban community college systems, and four years' work investigating aspects related to rural community colleges as part of two Ford Foundation–sponsored research grants.

Table 2.2 does not consider the private nonprofit, proprietary, tribal, or special use institutions. It should be noted that many of the potential research problems associated with rural community colleges, particularly those with enrollments below a thousand FTE students, likely apply to Tribal Colleges. Only one of the twenty-nine Tribal Colleges, Salish Kootenai College (Montana), has an enrollment approaching a thousand students. While there will be exceptions to these generalizations, which should be viewed only as hypotheses subject to further testing, it is still useful to describe these variances and the implications for community college leadership development, research, and policy formation.

Variations in Governance and Administration

There are major differences in the governance of rural, suburban, and urban community colleges. In general, rural community colleges are single-board, single-campus institutions, while urban community colleges are single-board, multicampus districts. Suburban community colleges tend to have a single board and a large student body (whether or not there is more than one campus). It follows, then, that the skills needed by chief executive officers and senior staff vary significantly across institutional types. Rural community college leaders have to be generalists as well as specialists. They must possess knowledge regarding accreditation, assessment, and state policies and procedures, and they must possess political, collective bargaining, and other skills. There is simply no one else to whom responsibilities can be delegated. The president must carry out a wide array of tasks and cannot be divorced from day-to-day administrative issues. This contrasts sharply with the situation at large suburban and urban community colleges, where sheer size requires decentralization. In multicampus districts, geography alone prevents the CEO

Table 2.2. Testable Hypotheses Regarding Diversity Among Public Community Colleges

	Rural	Suburban	Urban
Governance	single board, single campus	single board, single and multicampus	single board, generally multicampus
Nature of institution/ Skills needed by CEO	centralized generalist	more decentralized focused	highly decentralized focused
Access to local property taxes (percent)	low* (9–15)	highest* (21–22)	high* (14–17)
Physical plant challenge	refurbish older buildings	build new or expanded buildings	refurbish older buildings
Specialized staff	low or nonexistent	highly available	highly available
Student characteristics			
Sex	majority female	majority female	majority female
Race (percent white)	80–90*	75–90*	under 70* (often majority-minority)
Family history	mainly first generation	many first generation	vast majority first generation
Student aid	great need	large need	greatest need
Developmental education	great need	significant need	greatest need, including ESL
Curriculum	comprehensive	comprehensive	comprehensive except in small community colleges
Access to adjuncts	low or nonexistent	very high	very high
Workforce training and economic development emphasis	small manufacturers, entrepreneurship	large manufacturers and large firms	large and small manufacturers

Source: Developed by author from analysis of IPEDS data, except items marked (*), which are from Milam (1995).

from having direct administrative involvement. For example, Miami-Dade Community College's Homestead Campus is an hour and fifteen minute drive from the downtown district offices, making a decentralized approach to administration a necessity.

Do organizational culture and climate vary by community college type? It seems logical that such variation occurs. The need for good case studies employing rigorous qualitative research methods is as great for rural community colleges as it is for urban and suburban institutions. For example, Roueche and Baker's analysis (1987) of systems that foster student success at Miami-Dade Community College could be replicated at other types of institutions to provide a richer picture of the student experience at urban community colleges. The literature on community colleges could be strengthened if case studies and ethnographic analyses, such as those conducted by Clark (1960) or Weis (1985), were replicated in a variety of settings.

Are there significant differences based on geography between community colleges regarding availability of adjunct faculty and specialized staff? It seems logical that there would be. The shortage of well-trained grant writers at smaller rural based institutions is well known by practitioners in the field, but deficiencies related to staffing have not been empirically tested in the literature using comparable classifications.

Finance, Physical Plant, and Economic Development

Are there significant differences in terms of access to local property taxes among and between publicly controlled community colleges based upon geography? The *Pocket Profile of Community Colleges,* published jointly by the American Association of Community Colleges and the Association of Community College Trustees (1995), which analyzed National Center for Education Statistics data for 1992, revealed that 17.8 percent of total revenue for all community colleges came from local sources. Milam's (1995) analysis of 1990 IPEDS data suggests there are significant differences among and between community colleges. According to her analysis, suburban community colleges received the largest percentage—between 21 and 22 percent of their total income—from local tax sources (usually property taxes), followed by urban community colleges (about 17 percent), and rural community colleges (10 to 14 percent). Milam's analysis certainly should be tested by those interested in assessing finances and their relationship to social mobility provided by community colleges.

Additional evidence stems from participation by the writer in a Ford Foundation–sponsored research project examining issues, problems, and challenges faced by rural institutions in providing access and economic development. Site visits to nine of the ninety rural community colleges that serve the 319 severely economically distressed counties in the United States (as designated by the U.S. Department of Agriculture) revealed the tough circumstances these institutions face. Clustered in Appalachia, the lower Mississippi

Delta, the Four Corners region, the High Plains, and the Mexican Border region, these community colleges possessed such low property values that even large increases in local property taxes would produce only minuscule increases in revenue.

In an age of governmental devolution of responsibility from federal to state to local governments, does access to a solid local tax base matter? Does it relate to the capacity of types of community colleges to respond to challenges such as maintaining a high-quality, up-to-date physical plant, including the equipment to provide computer and Internet access? Is it more difficult for multicounty community college districts to pass local levies than for single-county districts? Many states, including Minnesota and Ohio, now require their community colleges to match state funds with institutional resources when constructing new facilities or refurbishing existing facilities. As state legislatures impose tuition caps on community colleges, what are the implications of these policies for different institutional settings, and can the assumptions behind those policies now be empirically tested?

Related to this is the issue of specialized staff in the area of financial management. Many rural community colleges are forced to train their own chief financial affairs officers, and do not have funds to provide adequate professional development opportunities for these individuals, placing their institutions at a disadvantage. Such costs are often hidden. Many publicly controlled rural community colleges do not employ bridge financing techniques that enable colleges to use the cash flow from their direct-support foundations to finance the acquisition, renovation, and refurbishing of physical plant facilities. One rural institution visited possessed an active foundation with more than enough cash flow to become engaged in projects using bridge financing. Yet it did not have staff with the specialized skills needed to assess institutional capacity to use such techniques. In contrast, Miami-Dade Community College financed nearly $43 million in facilities construction and renovation between 1985 and 1993 using Internal Revenue Service small bond regulations and other progressive financing techniques (Miami-Dade Community College Foundation, 1995, p. 17). Does access to such financing translate into qualitative differences for students using types of community colleges? With a classification system that recognizes differences in institutional settings, it is possible to test questions related to the varied skills possessed by community college chief financial officers or others in leadership roles.

Do rural, suburban, and urban community colleges differ in terms of their involvement with business and industry, and in their focus regarding economic development and workforce training? Logic would suggest so, but this hypothesis has not been empirically tested. Given research that shows that since 1970 many new large manufacturing plants have located in suburban areas, it would seem logical that geography would dictate the number of clients served and dollar volume of training contracts different types of community colleges have with business and industry. At rural community colleges that serve areas with few large firms, there may be fewer opportunities for large-scale training contracts and greater emphasis on serving small manufacturing enterprises. In contrast to suburban areas, there may be a stronger focus on the development of entrepreneurship at rural and inner-city community colleges to spur economic development. Again, such questions arise from looking at community colleges as highly varied institutions.

Student Characteristics

In terms of the student characteristics, there are common trends across college types. It is well known that the student body is majority female; however, are there differences based upon income and parental status of the female students served by community colleges of various types? That all types of community colleges serve significant numbers of first-generation students is also well known, but questions remain: Do urban community colleges serve a student body with significantly higher percentages of students on Title IV need-based student financial aid than other types of community colleges? Are there differences based upon race and ethnicity that correlate to other factors that might affect social mobility? Milam's (1995) analysis found that urban community colleges enrolled the largest numbers of minority students; do such differences correlate with other variables?

Are there significant differences among and between types of community colleges regarding the need for and type of development education provided? As Kempner and Kinnick (1990) point out, developmental education is necessary if American higher education is not to become what Temple and Polk (1986, p. 79) refer to as a "single elimination tournament." Do community colleges serving large numbers of nonnative speakers of English provide different kinds of developmental education services than other institutions?

In rural areas where reliable transportation is a necessary prerequisite to access, does the lack of public subsidized transit result in lower rates of attendance, degree completion, and transfer than in urban or suburban areas? These are but a few of the fascinating student issues that can be studied using agreed-upon institutional definitions.

Teaching and Learning Issues

Are there significant differences based on geography among and between community colleges in terms of comprehensive curriculum? General education and transfer offerings operate alongside technical, occupational, and vocational programs at virtually all publicly controlled community colleges. But there are clear differences in curricular breadth and depth related to size. Small rural colleges may have a limited capacity to offer wide-ranging curriculum, and a severely limited or nonexistent access to adjunct faculty. These institutions must carefully assess their local markets prior to determining if they should hire a faculty member in a vocational or general education area. They do not enjoy the luxury experienced by their urban and suburban counterparts of using adjuncts in the early years of a program to see if the offering takes root, building enrollments that can support the investment in full-time faculty positions.

Are there significant differences in transfer rates among and between types of community colleges? Again, we can logically assume that programs and services promoting transfer would be different for large, multicampus urban systems as compared to small, geographically isolated community colleges like Hazard Community College in rural eastern Kentucky. Is transfer partly related to depth and breadth of the curriculum offered? Does size matter? Small community colleges with enrollments under a thousand students often have difficulty in offering a wide menu of sophomore-level transfer courses such as organic chemistry, sophomore calculus, and preengineering or pre-science. A similar phenomenon can be found at the tribal colleges, nearly all of which enroll fewer than a thousand students. Logic supports the notion that institutional size matters, as urban and suburban community colleges can spread the cost of specialized offerings to a much larger potential student population than their small rural counterparts. Such questions beg further investigation.

Do larger institutions enjoy advantages in specialized computer and technical support, fund raising and grant development, institutional research, and specialized student support services staff? It is well known by practitioners that rural community colleges often have to develop and train their own specialized staff. In an age in which access to the Internet and other information age teaching and learning technologies is becoming increasingly important, what are the institutional differences in terms of faculty development support provided?

Implications of Classifications for Leadership Programs

This chapter argues that significant differences exist among and between community colleges that operate in various institutional settings. It outlines a Carnegie-style classification system for community colleges based upon objective data (geography, governance, and enrollment size), and poses a number of hypotheses that might be empirically tested. Students in graduate programs for community college leaders need to be exposed to the diversity in community college governance, finance, economic development, students, and curriculum issues; graduate programs need to emphasize diversity in community colleges rather than portray them in the aggregate. Empirical analysis of such questions can serve as a springboard to rich qualitative analysis of organizational culture, which in turn can inform both graduate and continuing education programs for community college leaders and practitioners in the field. This can bridge gaps in the literature that endure due to a lack of agreed-upon definitions of institutional types of community colleges, and assist researchers who write about community colleges from fields such as economics and sociology by providing a framework for understanding. Demonstrating the diversity that is well known by practitioners but perhaps overlooked by researchers is a way to bring greater intellectual substance and currency to graduate and continuing education programs involved in the preparation of community college leaders.

References

American Association of Community Colleges and Association of Community College Trustees. *Pocket Profile of Community Colleges: Trends and Statistics, 1995–1996.* Washington, D.C.: American Association of Community Colleges and Association of Community College Trustees, 1995

Breneman, D. W., and Nelson, S. C. *Financing Community Colleges: An Economic Perspective.* Washington, D.C.: Brookings Institution, 1981.

Bureau of the Census. *1990 Census of Population and Housing (CPH-2), and Press Releases (CB94–15).* Washington, D.C.: Bureau of the Census, 1990.

Bureau of the Census. *State and Metropolitan Area Data Book, 1991: A Statistical Abstract Supplement: Metropolitan Areas, Central Cities, and States.* (4th ed.) Washington, D.C.: Bureau of the Census, 1991.

Carnegie Foundation for the Advancement of Teaching. *A Classification of Institutions of Higher Education: A Technical Report.* Princeton, N.J.: Carnegie Foundation for the Advancement of Teaching, 1987.

Carnegie Foundation for the Advancement of Teaching. *A Classification of Institutions of Higher Education: A Technical Report.* Princeton, N.J.: Carnegie Foundation for the Advancement of Teaching, 1994.

Clark, B. *The Open Door College: A Case Study.* New York: McGraw-Hill, 1960.

Katsinas, S. "Toward a Classification System for Community Colleges." Paper presented at the annual meeting of the Council of Universities and Colleges, Portland, Oreg., Apr. 1993. (ED 377 925)

Kempner, K. "Toward a Classification of Community Colleges." Speech given at the 73rd Annual American Association of Community Colleges Convention, Apr. 28 to May 1, 1993, Portland, Oreg.

Kempner, K., and Kinnick, M. "Catching the Window: Being On Time for Higher Education." *Journal of Higher Education,* 1990, *61* (5), 535–547.

Miami-Dade Community College Foundation. *Annual Report 1995.* Miami, Fla.: Miami-Dade Community College Foundation, 1995.

Milam, P. "Toward a Classification System for Publicly Controlled Community Colleges." Unpublished doctoral dissertation in higher education administration, Oklahoma State University, 1995.

National Center for Education Statistics. *Integrated Postsecondary Education Data System (IPEDS).* Washington, D.C.: National Center for Education Statistics, 1994. Computer laser optical disks.

Roueche, J. E., and Baker, G. A., III. *Access and Excellence: The Open Door College.* Washington, D.C.: Community College Press, 1987.

Temple, M., and Polk, K. "A Dynamic Analysis of Educational Attainment." *Sociology of Education,* 1968, *59*(2), 79–84.

Weis, L. *Between Two Worlds: Black Students in an Urban Community College.* New York: Routledge, 1985.

STEPHEN G. KATSINAS is associate professor of higher education at the University of Toledo, Toledo, Ohio.

*The authors focus the debate on educating future community
college leaders by asserting the importance of writing skills.*

Educating Future Community
College Leaders as Skilled Writers:
Focusing the Debate

George B. Vaughan, Barbara Scott

Higher education emerged as an accepted field of study during the last half of
this century. As have professors in other fields of study, professors who teach
in graduate programs in higher education have spent countless hours debat-
ing what knowledge and skills students should possess before completing their
degrees. For the most part, the debate has centered on answering the following question: What skills and knowledge will contribute most to the graduate's
ability to lead an institution of higher education as a dean or as a president?
The answer to this question is especially important to the future of community colleges. If past is prologue to the future, these institutions will rely heavily on graduate programs in higher education to prepare their future leaders.

Certainly, examining the desirable skills and knowledge required for
future community college leaders and the role of higher education graduate
programs in developing those skills and providing that knowledge requires
more thought and discussion than can be captured in a single chapter, or in a
book, for that matter. Yet it is possible to focus the debate in ways that will
allow graduate professors of higher education to consider what, for many, will
be a new perspective when evaluating the effectiveness of their programs.

The following questions might help focus the debate regarding how one
should educate future community college leaders. First, and most obvious,
what should be the debate's focus? Second, why is this focus an important one?
Third, what should be expected of graduates of higher education programs in
relation to that focus? Finally, what role should the professoriate play in assur-
ing that those expectations are met?

Answers to these questions will, we hope, shed some light on the larger question: What skills and knowledge will be most helpful to future community college leaders?

Focusing the Debate

What is the role of the professoriate in developing the next generation of community college leaders? We feel that professors of higher education should spend as much time and energy as is required to assure that graduates of their programs write clearly, present their thoughts logically, and follow accepted rules of grammar and punctuation. This focus, we feel, is just as important as teaching students to design, conduct, and evaluate research, all of which are mandatory in effective doctoral programs, regardless of the field of study. These lessons hone a student's critical thinking skills. Likewise, the process of writing and revising one's writing involves examining one's thoughts and reordering them, when appropriate, to carry readers smoothly from one idea to the next. We would go so far as to suggest that students cannot be effective community college leaders without being able to write clearly, logically, and according to accepted rules. To focus the debate on the issue of writing will, we believe, require professors of higher education to view what constitutes an effective graduate program from a perspective that is often missing.

The Importance of the Debate

Effective writing is the skill that future community college leaders are likely to need and use more than any other. One community college professional, in commenting on community college students, notes that too often students avoid disciplines they will need most of their lives, "such as written communication skills." These skills constitute "the basic fibre from which their feelings are examined and their thoughts are formed" (Lanier, 1995, p. 35). Writing skills—which involve being able to examine one's thoughts and feelings and to convey them effectively—are essential to leaders in any profession. Community college leaders must represent their institutions to the public and to their colleagues in higher education. The ability to write effectively enables a college leader to explain the institution's mission to the public and engage in scholarly discourse about higher education.

Writing is a way to portray one's thoughts, and a disorganized document that is riddled with inconsistencies makes an unfavorable impression on its readers. The author of "The Manager's Journal" in the Wall Street Journal notes the importance of orderly writing: "Of all the writing problems that plague business people, none is more far-reaching or likely to cripple profits and profitability than lack of organization. Documents that meander usually fail in their attempt to either inform or persuade" (Blake, 1995, p. A-14).

Moreover, a recent article in the New York Times mentioned a study conducted at Bell Laboratories to determine which characteristics marked successful engineers. It noted that "the most valued and productive engineers" were not those with the most intelligence, the best academic credentials, or the highest scores on their achievement tests. The most valued engineers were those whose *congenial expressiveness* "put them at the heart of the informal communication networks that would spring up during times of crisis or innovation" (Goleman, 1995).

In other words, the engineers described in the study were both congenial and expressive: They established their willingness to cooperate with others who shared the same communication networks, and they expressed their ideas and feelings in an agreeable and effective manner. When these engineers e-mailed for help, they received instant answers from an on-line community. Others online sometimes waited days or weeks for replies (Goleman, 1995). The engineers with congenial expressiveness had established themselves as perceptive and effective communicators via an electronic network that relied on written messages. Their writing elicited responses from a community of readers.

Is the ability to compose expressive messages important to our graduates? An article in *Community College Week* discussed a recent survey of desktop computing conducted by Kenneth Green at the University of Southern California. The survey indicated that community college access to the Internet doubled between 1992 and 1994 and that approximately 75 percent of two-year colleges were connected to the Internet (Cross, 1994a). Other news items point to the Internet's growing importance as a tool for community college educators. For example, the League for Innovation has established an electronic Discussion Forum on Educational Technologies (Cross, 1994b). Other such forums are sure to follow in the years ahead. The leaders of our educational institutions may find in the near future that their professional advancement will depend on their ability to work effectively in the electronic community and to elicit responses from others through their writing.

Physical charm and professional status carry little weight in the electronic community, as noted in a recent article in *Time* magazine: "Stripped of the external trappings of wealth, power, beauty, and social status, people tend to be judged in the cyberspace of the Internet only by their ideas and their ability to get them across in terse, vigorous prose" (Elmer-DeWitt, 1995, p. 9). What does the ability to write terse and vigorous prose involve?

What We Should Expect of Graduates

To write well, one must understand the mechanics of grammar and punctuation. Some writers (but certainly not graduate students) are fortunate enough to have an astute assistant or copyeditor to handle the details of grammar and punctuation. But many leaders must produce their own letters, reports, and scholarly manuscripts. The fine details of grammar and punctuation may escape the average reader's eye, but obvious errors stand out in written documents. The errors that stand out are immediately recognized because they sound or look wrong as they are read: inconsistencies in subject and verb agreement, obvious misspellings, incomplete sentences, and the displacement or lack of punctuation. Graduates of higher education programs must learn to recognize these errors and to correct them according to accepted rules of grammar and punctuation.

Learning the rules for avoiding the most obvious grammatical mistakes is not difficult. Doing so means that one can present a document that does not distract the reader with obvious errors. But this ability alone does not qualify one as a competent writer. A competent writer is one who understands the assumptions that underlie the way we use language.

Both speaking and writing rest upon some important assumptions: We assume that speakers and writers will use language that is appropriate to a situation or context. They will cooperate with others by giving enough information to make their messages understood and by offering relevant information. Further, effective speakers and writers all know that they are expected to follow accepted rules of manner and order in their messages and that they are expected to be truthful (Finegan, 1994, p. 342). Those who violate these principles of communication take the risk of being viewed as inappropriate, befuddled, lacking in social manner, or unreliable.

Imagine your feelings when you greet someone you barely know. If the customary greeting of "How are you?" is returned with a detailed summary of the other's physical, mental, and emotional state, you sense immediately that the rule of appropriateness has been violated. Similarly, when you ask someone a question about a particular topic, you assume that you will receive a truthful answer about that topic. You expect a response that will contain enough information to answer your question. In other words, you expect an answer that is relevant, concise, and honest.

Although both speaking and writing rely on these same assumptions, they differ in some important ways. The spoken word is accompanied by gestures, stance, gaze, and facial movements. What one says is reinforced by voice—intonation, stress, and volume. All these characteristics of spoken language combine to communicate both an obvious spoken message and other unspoken messages such as "It's my turn to speak" (Finegan, 1994). Conversation allows speakers to adjust their messages spontaneously based upon a listener's reactions. An ill-timed comment can be withdrawn or ameliorated, and a statement made with less than adequate information can be amended.

Unless recorded with video or audio equipment, spoken communication has "an evanescent character" (Finegan, 1994, p. 18). Though spoken words may linger in someone's memory, they disappear once they are uttered. They are not subject to the same kind of scrutiny that formal recorded speeches and written documents must endure.

Moreover, written messages rely solely on words and their arrangement (along with typography and punctuation) for their effect. Writers cannot use stance, gestures, facial expressions, and intonation to convey any subtle information that might lie beneath the surface of their messages. Nor can they adjust their messages in response to such cues from their audiences. Writers must achieve tone and expression solely through the use of grammar and syntax (Finegan, 1994, pp. 379–380), and they must discern an audience's needs and expectations beforehand.

Anticipating an audience's needs and defining the context for a written document requires sensitivity to people's expectations and the ability to adapt one's writing style to fit the situation (Gaitens, 1994, pp. 3–6). For instance, scholarly writing—the writing our graduate students must produce—focuses on a topic and uses a prescribed formal style. On the other hand, the professional writing required of educational leaders focuses on its readers and the information they need to solve a problem or understand an issue. Professional writing runs the gamut from formal letters and reports to casual memos, so its style depends upon the message's form.

Graduate students must realize that any document they produce, be it a memo, a letter, or a formal report to the governing board, becomes a permanent record of their competence and sensitivity as communicators. Those who write well make known their ability to perceive what kind of information (and how much of it) is appropriate and relevant in many different situations. They convey that they know how to interpret professional situations with sensitivity and skill, and they demonstrate that they know the accepted rules of manner, truthfulness, and order that govern communication.

A scholarly article about a research project or a report to a board of trustees allows the writer to go through the steps of planning the document, creating an initial draft, and editing it to his or her satisfaction (Gaitens, 1994, p. 4). Planned documents give the writer time to discern the appropriate language and to gather the right amounts and kinds of information. The writer has time to organize the document and to ensure that its order and style fulfill the required purpose, and also has time to check the accuracy of the facts presented, to ensure truthfulness. Graduate students must learn how to maneuver through each of the steps required to create effective documents.

Such planned writing situations give writers several opportunities to alter documents and present their communication abilities in the best light. Being able to demonstrate these abilities spontaneously will become more important as our institutions and their leaders join the growing electronic community. Whether through everyday e-mail communication or through one of the online discussion groups that are part of the Internet, our leaders will be represented (and judged) at times solely by the quality of their prose.

The engineers described by Goleman who had established themselves as congenial and expressive on an e-mail network accomplished much with their written messages. They encountered situations described to them, interpreted them sensitively, and responded appropriately. Their messages elicited attention and provoked responses. As communicators, these engineers certainly understood the foundations upon which language rests: appropriateness, relevance, conciseness, and honesty. They convinced others of their willingness to cooperate and of their reliability with what Elmer-DeWitt calls "terse, vigorous prose."

Creating such prose is any writer's task, regardless of the writing situation. The ability to write well—to convey with words alone that one understands a situation and that one is truthful and cooperative—has always been an important aspect of leadership. Before the telephone became an important way to convey messages, the written word was more important than it has been in recent times. Appropriateness, relevance, conciseness, and truthfulness were essential when written messages constituted much of the business and scholarly communication that took place.

Will technology resurrect the importance of writing well? It already has for those who are joining the electronic community. And as we have noted, becoming a part of that community is inevitable for community college faculty and administrators.

Those who can demonstrate with the quality of their writing that they understand the foundations of communication—appropriateness, relevance, conciseness, and truthfulness—will become the leaders of the electronic community. Those who write well are likely to lead in their chosen professions as well.

The Role of the Professoriate

Perhaps the most important role professors of higher education can play in teaching graduate students to write clearly, present their thoughts effectively, and follow accepted rules of grammar and punctuation is to follow these practices themselves and work to see that other members of the profession do the same. Are we stating the obvious? We think not. Are graduate professors guilty of being less than clear and logical in their writing and in recommending writings that suffer from the same shortcomings? We think so, at least more often than is desirable. Most writers have lapses in their writing at times, including the authors of this discussion. Nevertheless, professors must work to assure that graduate students can tell the difference between good and poor writing.

How can professors help students to distinguish between what is acceptable writing and what is not? Professors must let graduate students know that their writing must be clear, orderly, and in accordance with accepted rules. Standards must be stated clearly and enforced in every piece of writing that students submit for evaluation. If rewrites are needed, they must be required, with the professor providing guidance. If graduate professors are unwilling to establish and uphold standards of writing, it is unlikely that students will understand the need for high standards in their own writing.

One way of achieving an acceptable level of writing is to have students read the works of others, including the works assigned for class, with a critical eye. Graduate professors in higher education are often hesitant to criticize their colleagues' writing, especially in front of graduate students. Several steps can be taken to assure the students that it is the writing, not the individual, being criticized.

The professor can reinforce the necessity of critical analysis in any scholarly undertaking, pointing out that criticism (a word that has undeservedly taken on negative connotations) is a necessary part of any graduate program worth its salt. Examples of the professor's own writing can be among the first to be criticized. Other examples of both good and poor writing should be examined and criticized; although most graduate students are intelligent enough to know when something is written well, they often have not developed the critical skills required to analyze what is wrong with poor or ineffective writing.

Students should learn to ask some basic questions as they analyze their own writing and that of other writers: Does each sentence contain one idea, rather than two or three? A reader should be able to understand one idea before moving to the next. Do the ideas that the sentences represent follow each other logically? Transitional words can help a reader make connections, but the connections between thoughts must be present. Are any terms that are not commonly known defined? If not, a reader might misinterpret the writer's intended meaning. Are sources cited for information that is not commonly known? It is especially important to document sources for quotations and statistical information.

Graduate students who have been taught to document everything often take the advice literally. For example, the following statement (paraphrased) is taken from an article found in a popular book of readings on the community college: "The community college, with its vast resources, is uniquely qualified to meet a number of community needs." The author of the article lists two sources documenting the statement—a statement that requires no documentation.

Part of teaching students to write effectively includes teaching them to distinguish between what is common knowledge and what needs documentation. Too many graduate students have developed the habit of sprinkling their writings with citations, whether needed or not, in an effort to appear scholarly. Professors must teach students to judge when citations are required and when they are unnecessary.

Students should analyze their reading assignments for elements of clarity, logic, and accepted rules of grammar and punctuation. To sharpen their critical skills before turning to semester papers and dissertation proposals, students should write short documents based on what they have learned about writing. These discussions, which can be integrated into most graduate classes, should then be subjected to the criticism of other graduate students, with the faculty member offering guidance when appropriate.

Two authors, one of whom teaches in a graduate program in higher education, argue in the *Chronicle of Higher Education's* "Point of View" column that faculty members should become more involved in teaching students how to write. "As is the case with other skills, writing requires coaching and practice for improvement, and faculty members must be willing to provide this instruction" (Wagener and Lazerson, 1995, p. A60). To this admonition, we would add that writing also requires criticism for improvement. One message that should be conveyed to graduate students is that criticism is something one should seek, understand, and appreciate. No one can learn to write well in a vacuum.

Finally, any writing submitted for a class or a dissertation should be critically evaluated by professors. It is a rare paper or dissertation indeed that does not suffer to some degree from lack of clarity: sentences that contain more ideas than a reader can easily digest, connected by strings of prepositional phrases and containing terms that are vaguely defined (or not defined at all). Teaching students to take their writing apart and to view it critically teaches them to analyze their thinking as well—to take apart and reorder a sequence of thoughts and to define the key concepts. Effective writing is often difficult to achieve without criticism from someone else. Rarely do students use grammar and punctuation perfectly. For us to fail to note these shortcomings is to abandon a part of our responsibility as graduate professors. Failure to write well will result in graduates who fail to achieve their potential as leaders.

Summary

The debate on how we should educate future community college leaders has many facets, and we focused on the importance of writing well. Writing is a fundamental skill that community college leaders must use often in the contexts of everyday correspondence, scholarly research, and reports to the governing boards and to the communities they serve. Now that technology allows us to exchange messages with a widening sphere of other professionals who have like interests and problems, the importance of writing well will increase. Our graduate students must learn to transfer the skills they use in their everyday conversation to writing. They must learn to analyze the needs of their audiences and to interpret the demands of different writing situations, just as they automatically adjust their conversational style and content in different speaking situations. They must learn to write well spontaneously if they are to participate in the immediate exchange of information that is becoming an everyday part of the workplace, including the community college.

We close with a note of caution. Critiquing students' writing to help them learn to organize and convey their thoughts more effectively does not mean that we should discriminate against or judge those who cannot write well. Many students who enter graduate programs have navigated an educational system that may not have prepared them for this task. Many students have learned English as a second language. Their writing may not in any way reflect their intelligence or their potential for accomplishment. Unfortunately, a student's intelligence and potential may be judged by others as lacking because he or she does not write effectively and appropriately in a given situation. If students leave our graduate programs without an understanding of what it takes to write effectively, they leave with a handicap. Indeed, their graduate program may be their last chance to get the structured criticism they need to become conscious of their writing strengths and weaknesses. We must not fail them at this stage of their education.

References

Blake, G. "It Is Recommended That You Write Clearly." The Managers Journal. *Wall Street Journal*, Apr. 3, 1995, p. A-14.

Cross, C. "Community Colleges Lead in Classroom Use of Computers, Survey Shows." *Community College Week*, Nov. 21, 1994a, p. 9.

Cross, C. "Computer Conference Demonstrates Future for Community Colleges." *Community College Week*, Dec. 5, 1994b, p. 11.

Elmer-DeWitt, P. "Welcome to Cyberspace." *Time*, 1995, *145* (12), 4–11.

Finegan, E. *Language: Its Structure and Use.* (2nd ed.) Orlando: Harcourt Brace, 1994.

Gaitens, J. *Communication for Business and Management: Resource Packet.* Raleigh: North Carolina State University, 1994.

Goleman, D. "Broader Measure of IQ Identified." *News & Observer,* Sept. 17, 1995, pp. 23A, 30A.

Lanier, S. "This Is English." *FOCUS: A Forum on Teaching and Learning in Utah Community Colleges,* 1995, *12,* 35–36.

Wagener, U., and Lazerson, M. "The Faculty's Role in Fostering Student Learning." *Chronicle of Higher Education,* Oct. 6, 1995, p. A60.

GEORGE B. VAUGHAN is associate director of the Academy for Community College Leadership Advancement, Innovation, and Management, editor of the Community College Review, *and a professor in the Department of Adult and Community College Education at North Carolina State University, Raleigh.*

BARBARA SCOTT is managing editor of the Community College Review *in the Department of Adult and Community College Education at North Carolina State University, Raleigh.*

The problems posed by the ever-changing environments in which community college leaders work place great demands on their capacity to understand and analyze problems related to personnel management, organizational development, adult learning, technology, community relations, facilities, finance, and (not least) personal development.

The Door That Never Closes: Continuing Education Needs of Community College Leaders

Joseph N. Hankin

Wanted: Educator with doctorate, evidence of being on top of current-day issues, and possession of the following attributes: ability to capitalize on ambiguity, ability to anticipate situations, a proactive orientation to problems, knowledge of how organizations work, experience in mentoring others to leadership, and experience in creating structures and bureaucracies that make things happen. In addition, the candidate will have demonstrated skills in program planning, decision making, marketing, communications, financial planning, fiscal management, psychology, sociology, statistical analysis, and strategic planning. He or she will be skilled in conflict resolution, stress management, listening, and delegation and organization. He or she will be tactful but firm, react well to frustration, and demonstrate social sensitivity. Other attributes to be discussed.

Does this advertisement sound fantastic? Perhaps so, but increasingly, this is the kind of person search committees and institutions seek. Of course, no one person can fulfill all attributes equally, but rarely does the employing body take the position that all the skills must be represented collectively among members of the leadership team rather than individually within the person of the president. Search committees expect a superman or superwoman!

In the face of these expectations, many newly minted administrators bewail the fact that their graduate education programs have not prepared them for the real world. They have been exposed to standard courses and content, but rarely to current issues in collective bargaining, sexual harassment, administrative ethics, and other vital areas. Moreover, other, more subtle, skills and attributes are needed for advancement. Where are they taught? How are they learned? How can professionals keep abreast of the changing environment, and do they receive support from their own institutions to do so?

The problem of preparing for and keeping up with the real world is not unique to the field of community college education. However, it is of immediate import to two-year college educators, who must respond to continual changes in the social, demographic, and economic conditions of their local service districts. Just as the lights in the classroom building shine for our students at all hours of the day and night, those who administer programs in these buildings require regular rejuvenation or enlightenment. Graduate programs alone do not pretend to educate administrators for a lifetime—but they can teach these same administrators to continue to learn on their own (Nowlen, 1988).

A requisite, however, is continued dialogue between university personnel and practicing community college educators. Just as community college educators are required to examine consumer needs when building instructional programs, so too must graduate schools communicate with practicing administrators in an attempt to determine how education might be effectively provided in ways that will last a lifetime, with periods out for renewal. The need is urgent, for as Rippey (1993, p. 215) notes, "there has been a growing perception [in recent years] that researchers, who are supposed to feed the professional schools with useful knowledge, have less and less to say that practitioners find useful."

This chapter offers an exploratory outline of the issues and concerns about which community college leaders may require further education or information. It is highly practical, based on the author's experience—including thirty years as a community college president—as well as on an informal poll of dozens of community college leaders and university educators nationwide. Results are reported in terms of philosophy, mission, goals, and objectives; students; programs and services; and personnel and organization.

Philosophy, Mission, Goals, and Objectives

Practitioners in the community college field say that we sometimes seem to grow without purpose, that we leap to every temptation without a plan. Part of the problem lies in the complex decision-making environment in which administrators operate. Cohen and Associates (1975, p. 79) put it well:

> Who decides how the resources will be allocated, which programs will be supported and which will not? Will the decisions be made by the customers of the College (the students), by the instructors through collective bargaining contracts, by administrators, by government officials, or by university professors? Will economic influences such as changing job requirements or the competition from proprietary schools influence decisions? What will be the effect of various social phenomena such as changing life styles? Undoubtedly, all will have some effect, but will some voices be louder than others?

Some training in decision making and program planning within this complex environment is clearly in order. Information on administrative theory that is usually gained in graduate classes can be useful, even vital. But the complicated environments in which administrators work generally interfere with a swift transition from theory to practice. Indeed, the administrators polled by the author continually stressed the need for a comfortable balance between theory and practice. What they learn in graduate school must have applicability, and what they learn on the job must be brought back somehow into the graduate school curriculum.

Another concern expressed by many of the individuals who were polled is the perceived need for more information on the history of community colleges and on the social context of the education these institutions provide. Community college educators are concerned that if they cannot state or describe the functions and missions of their institutions, they will be unable to inform external publics of what the community college contributes. Continual reflection on what we do and why we do it would seem highly appropriate. The analysis in Chapter One, which traces the development of graduate programs for community college leaders in the post–World War II years, is an example of the type of reflective thinking that is required, shedding light on where we are going by reminding us of where we have been.

Students

How often have you posed the question "How many students do you have?" only to hear a response that excludes noncredit students? This is ironic, not only because of the large number of noncredit students enrolled in community colleges, but also because the community college ostensibly adheres to a comprehensive educational philosophy. Despite this philosophy, professionals in the field often question the degree of success they have in providing nontraditional students with a range of services that is on a par with the services provided to on-campus, credit—so-called regular—students.

According to the professionals polled by the author, community college practitioners must thoroughly think through the question of who their clientele are. We give lip service, they say, to lifelong learning, but then write off the older, nontraditional students, treating them at best as a source of revenue. However, people continue to learn throughout their lives, and the task of the community college is to ascertain when they most need learning, what they need, and how that learning should be provided.

Some in the field suggest that community colleges should compare their student populations with the population profiles of their service areas. Programs might then be developed in ways that enhance the match between curriculum and local community needs. Colleges will be successful to the extent that differences between the general population and the student population are minimized.

The future-oriented college will continue to serve or seek new populations, preferably as an extension of a coherent educational philosophy and not simply out of fear that continued existence of the college is contingent on enrollment growth. As traditional student populations shrink, there will be increasing pressure on colleges to bring in new populations and new students. How to do that is a felt need of those who are current practitioners. Practitioners need to be able to analyze demographic trends, identify unmet needs, segment markets, write motivational advertising copy, conduct direct mail campaigns. All are areas that could be the focus of continuing education efforts.

Practitioners also need a greater understanding of adult life cycles and the role education plays in the lives of adults. In 1980, Aslanian and Brickell wrote *Americans in Transition: Life Changes as Reasons for Adult Learning,* which was followed in 1988 by *How Americans in Transition Study for College Credit.* The first book concluded that adults learn in order to cope with changes in their lives, and the authors list a series of specific events that trigger these transitions; examples include getting hired or fired, getting married or divorced, having children, getting sick, getting elected to public office, or moving to a new city. Although occupational needs are predominant motivators for continuing education, these events also play large roles in converting adults from latent to active learners. (The 1980 study investigated why and when adults study but it did not address how they learn; hence the sequel book.) Those in the field say they need to understand these motivations, as well as how adults learn and how colleges can use this information to build appropriate programs, courses, and services. Books such as those by Aslanian and Brickell are very important sources of continuing education for community college educators.

Programs and Services

Community colleges face growing competition, not only from standard competitors such as proprietary institutions, but from a panoply of community service agencies that also provide educational services and programs. The wide variety of community-based agencies offering educational services is well documented by Merriam and Cunningham (1989). Many of the learning opportunities they provide seem to be designed to meet immediate learning needs in a short period of time. Community college professionals polled by the author profess a desire to learn how to assess these needs and then translate the information gained through such assessments into meaningful programs for their clients.

This is especially critical in light of the criticism community colleges often receive for poor curriculum planning. Courses are sometimes offered on little more than the hunch of a staff member with scant information on their long-range value. Programs or courses may be planned on a hit-or-miss basis rather than around some organizing principle. Recognizing these criticisms, practitioners in the field express the need for training in the techniques of needs assessment and program analysis. (In this regard, Queeney's [1995] discussion of needs assessment in adult education is very helpful.) Practitioners also express a need for information on how to build programs with teams made up of faculty members and client representatives.

Finally, issues scanning in general is a primary concern, reflecting the need community college educators have for more information on the issues that are of concern to the populations they serve. The appropriate and meaningful inclusion of specific subjects in the curriculum, such as globalism and multi-culturalism, represents a related challenge that administrators must be pre-pared for. In short, community college practitioners need to continually learn about the methods and practices that link changing client needs with college curricula, thereby solidifying the college's niche in the adult education market.

Personnel and Organization

The educators polled by the author indicate that some of the severest critics of the community college are traditionally trained faculty members who do not accept the community college philosophy or who secretly attempt to remake it in their own image. These faculty members see in the community college movement a watering down of formal academic offerings. They seize on every report that is critical of two-year colleges and fear that many community col-lege offerings and services may not be appropriate for an institution of higher learning. On some campuses, regular faculty members see themselves as draftees when asked to participate in community or continuing education. Some faculty members resent the allocation of resources to noncredit programs, arguing instead that funds should be used in the so-called regular program.

How to deal with such attitudes worries many administrators, especially when personnel matters are subject to collective bargaining. Certainly some administrators feel that the stipulations of union contracts can be somewhat frustrating with respect to faculty selection or disciplinary proceedings. Many also feel that contracts can thwart a quick response to employer and commu-nity needs. Administrators would clearly welcome continuing education opportunities that address the problems of dealing with difficult employees or fostering team development under these circumstances. Techniques in conflict resolution should be stressed.

The need for conflict resolution skills arises not only from personnel prob-lems but from intraorganizational conflicts as well. Indeed, the poll of practi-tioners suggests that the juxtaposition of some units of the college against the rest of the organization makes life uncomfortable for some administrators, and they express the need to be able to cope with such conflicts. (See Heermann, 1980, pp. 89–90, for a discussion of the value of a centralized office versus fac-ulty or departmental control.) Multiple unions add to the complexity of the college's political arena. Where many faculty members work part time, the issue of their possible overuse has been raised. Sometimes this has led part-timers to organize unions that compete with the unions for full-time instruc-tors. Administrators need to understand and cope with these and other potentially contentious aspects of organizational life.

New issues come to the fore in interpersonal and human relations all the time. Administrators who graduated from programs in the 1960s often felt unprepared for collective bargaining, contract administration, the women's revolution, the civil rights movement, and emerging legal issues in such areas as affirmative action or sexual harassment. Changes in the administrative arena constantly outstrip experience and formal learning. Hence it becomes important to develop fundamental leadership skills: how to listen, how to read and comprehend varying points of view, how to organize, how to delegate, how to follow up, and even how to cope with frustration. All are essential to survival and growth.

In considering the professional development of leaders, it is also important to ask if we are paying enough attention to our aging administration. Are we properly attending to their renewal and professional growth, or are we treating them like a disposable resource that can be thrown away when we are finished with them? Although efforts are under way in most progressive community colleges to help faculty members serve lifelong learners (Christensen, 1980), one wonders if we are making comparable efforts to help administrators attend to the new challenges they face. Indeed, it would appear that formal professional development activities for faculty outnumber the professional development opportunities that are made available to administrators. The least we can do for the administrators who must help make our programs effective is to analyze their needs and provide the continuing education they need to keep themselves alive.

Instruction

We will not be able to do things as we did them yesterday. McLuhan (1964) has said that the anxiety of our age is, in great part, the result of trying to do today's job with yesterday's tools and with yesterday's concepts. This is certainly true of teaching. We now have two-way interactive cable television, home computers, and other marvelous learning devices—and more are on the way (Marshall, 1993). This does not mean that we must change our instructional techniques for the sake of change. But we must recognize that more and more of our customers have been brought up using visual media; their personal and economic lives involve the use of such technologies as home shopping networks, facsimile reproduction, and videocassette recorders.

Besides offering potential changes in the mode of instructional delivery for students who are increasingly used to electronic media, new technologies can help colleges reach out to their constituencies in different ways. Several colleges have television as well as radio stations on their campuses. Cable television connections and computer hookups make computer-assisted instruction accessible to students in a variety of campus or home locations; some courses are already taught via Lotus Notes and the Internet. Garrison (1989) has described these and many other forms of distance learning.

In addition, it is possible to tape faculty audio messages, course teasers, and whole segments of courses on cassettes for distribution to students. Institutions might even offer "cassette colleges." Some are exploring the medium of telephone tapes, which currently give information to callers on subjects of law, medicine, and consumer issues; why not use this technology to deliver courses? Many colleges already have the capacity to link the telephone and the computer in ways that allow older students to register without having to come to the campus. Given this capacity, it is logical for educators to consider its use in educational delivery; why not, they ask, use the same media to give instruction at a nursing home or for local shut-ins? We boast now about our weekend courses, our 7 A.M. courses for workers on the way to their places of employment, and our courses given in-plant for factory workers on a night shift. But think how much more we could do with the new technologies. Despite the possibilities, understanding and realizing the potential of these technologies leaves many administrators at sea. Most were trained and educated in more traditional times and in traditional educational settings. They need help in this area if the promise of the technological age is to be realized.

Other Managerial Concerns

In addition to problems related to mission, students, programs, personnel, and instruction, the administrators canvassed by the author mentioned a panoply of other concerns. Some are managerial in nature, while others relate to the skills and temperaments that foster administrative success.

Community use of facilities. One concern deals with the use of facilities to help solve community problems or assist in economic development efforts. Campus libraries, for example, may be increasingly open to the public, and several colleges may establish public library branches on their campuses. Similarly, computer resources will be available for hire by small businesses that cannot afford their own, and faculty in the computer sciences, business, and other areas may lend their expertise to local entrepreneurs as consultants. College administrators clearly need to develop methods of weighing competing demands for the use of institutional resources and allocating those resources in ways that make the greatest contribution to community life.

Finances. Administrators often complain about their lack of training in fiscal matters and their limited capacity to respond to critics who claim that "philosophy follows finances" or that resources are devoted to frivolous courses. (Parnell's 1982 essay, "Will Belly Dancing Be Our Nemesis?" well described the latter problem.) They therefore express a great need for further education in financial planning and management and in the politics of public funding. There is also a substantial need for a sharper understanding of budgetary techniques. Indeed, administrators complain that financial staff like to obscure fiscal matters in arcane ways, making it difficult for others to interpret budget figures. Administrators need to tackle this problem with the understanding that budgets are educational programs written out in dollar figures.

Cooperative relations with other agencies. Partly to stretch resources and partly to fulfill mission, community colleges cooperate with a variety of local agencies (including proprietary schools, public schools, businesses, and civic groups) in ways that guard against proliferation of programs, fragmentation of services, lack of coordination, and excessive competition. Unfortunately, how-ever, too many institutions still go it alone, reflecting the need for administra-tors to become aware of the possibilities for collaboration and to take the lead in forging ties with community agencies. Community college administrators should be at the forefront of these efforts. Whatever the issue—adult literacy, racial harmony, or economic development—there is nothing stopping the col-lege from proposing the establishment of regional clearinghouses, initiating community needs analyses, or recommending ways of allocating scarce com-munity resources. College leaders, however, must be informed, willing to act, and skilled in the ways of effective organization.

Personal attributes. Finally, there are several personal attributes to which aspir-ing administrators must pay attention. A leading researcher in this area is Colum-bia University's Sharon McDade, who is currently interviewing fifty presidents to ascertain the steps they made in their "leadership learning journey" (Sharon McDade, personal communication, 12 February 1996). She asserts that leaders develop along several continua. One, for example, might be characterized as fol-lows: "Passive orientation to problems, active orientation to problems, proactive orientation to problems." Another relates to self-image: "Thinking of one's self as a worker, as a manager, as a leader . . . acting as a leader, mentoring others to lead-ership." When she has completed her research, faculty members and administra-tors may have a better road map for continuing education, one that suggests vectors of personal development as well as skills that need to be honed.

Conclusion

Those who administer continuing education enterprises, including community colleges, come from a variety of backgrounds. But the one thing they have in com-mon is the need to update their education on a regular basis. As the preceding discussion indicates, the problems posed by the ever-changing environments in which administrators work place great demands on their capacity to understand and analyze problems related to personnel management, organizational devel-opment, adult learning, technology, community relations, facilities, finance, and (not least) personal development. The range of required learning is enormous.

Ironically, however, little or no attention has been paid over the decades to continuing education for community college professionals. Merriam and Cunningham (1989), along with other practitioners and researchers, have con-cluded that just as colleges study everything but themselves, so too do practi-tioners of continuing education provide for the further education of everybody but themselves. The same may be said for community college leaders, whose business is continuing education but whose own professional careers often lack sufficient opportunities for formal learning and renewal.

Much of that learning can be accomplished through a disciplined read-ing program and through participation in the numerous professional devel-opment opportunities that are provided by universities and professional organizations, as described in Chapter Five. Policymakers can encourage this continuing education. In Florida, for example, statutes require public colleges to devote 2 percent of their educational and general revenues to faculty and staff development (Stephen G. Katsinas, personal communication, 5 December 1995). But given today's uncertain fiscal environment, other states are unlikely to follow Florida's lead.

It seems likely, therefore, that much of the initiative for continuing education must come from the university graduate programs that prepare community college leaders in the first place. Besides providing an intellectual foundation for these leaders, they can cooperate with community colleges and professional associations in meeting the learning needs that emerge as administrators face new problems. For example, North Carolina State University augments its graduate degree programs with (among other opportunities) workshops in the field and with a summer institute for community college leaders (William Deegan, personal communication, 30 June 1995). As another example, the University of South Carolina has worked with staff from the state's technical college system to provide a six-course continuing education program for staff and faculty; at least one of the courses has been delivered as an interactive telecourse (Bower, 1996).

These initiatives are fully in line with Rippey's (1993) observation that "the boundary between a profession and a professional school needs to be more permeable" (p. 218). University professors who teach graduate courses should be encouraged to augment credit instruction with participation in the planning and delivery of continuing education opportunities for community college practitioners. For this to happen, faculty reward structures—which often do not place a high priority on this participation—will have to be reconsidered.

If they do not already do so, university graduate schools should also build into their programs a realization that learning never ends. But without leadership from presidents and other administrators in the field who are themselves alumni of those programs, graduate school efforts to enhance continuing education opportunities may be an uphill battle. Campion (1994) put it well, pointing out that "continual efforts for presidential renewal and invigoration are absolutely necessary," and that "quality leaders arm themselves with a well fortified arsenal of renewal activities" (p. 166). He goes on to write that "in a well functioning, dynamic institution, the CEO must make certain that all other administrators are aware of and actively participating in staff development activities. . . . If the president fails to make certain that the institution's important administrators are actively involved in renewal activities, he or she can know with certainty that the institution will stagnate" (p. 167). Administrators occasionally forget this obligation. When they do, it is up to the graduate programs that prepare them in the first place to remind them.

References

Aslanian, C., and Brickell, H. *Americans in Transition: Life Changes as Reasons for Learning.* New York: College Entrance Examination Board, 1980.

Aslanian, C. and Brickell, H. *How Americans in Transition Study for College Credit.* New York: College Entrance Examination Board, 1988.

Bower, B. "A Carolina Education Partnership." *Community College Journal,* 66(6), 1996, 32–34.

Campion, W. J. "Providing for Avenues of Renewal." *Community College Journal of Research and Practice,* 1994, *18* (2), 165–176.

Christensen, F. "Equipping Faculty to Serve Lifelong Learners." In B. Heermann, C. C. Enders, and E. Wine (eds.), *Serving Lifelong Learners.* New Directions for Community Colleges, no. 29. San Francisco: Jossey-Bass, 1980.

Cohen, A. M., and Associates. *College Responses to Community Demands.* San Francisco: Jossey-Bass, 1975.

Garrison, D. R. "Distance Education." In S. B. Merriam and P. M. Cunningham (eds.), *Handbook of Adult and Continuing Education.* San Francisco: Jossey-Bass, 1989.

Heermann, B. "On Transforming a Traditional College." In B. Heermann, C. C. Enders, and E. Wine (eds.), *Serving Lifelong Learners.* New Directions for Community Colleges, no. 29. San Francisco: Jossey-Bass, 1980.

McLuhan, M. *Understanding Media.* New York: McGraw-Hill, 1964.

Marshall, J. G. "The Expanding Use of Technology." In L. Curry, J. F. Wergin, and Associates, *Educating Professionals: Responding to New Expectations for Competence and Accountability.* San Francisco: Jossey-Bass, 1993.

Merriam, S. B., and Cunningham, P. M. (eds.). *Handbook of Adult and Continuing Education.* San Francisco: Jossey-Bass, 1989.

Nowlen, P. M. *A New Approach to Continuing Education for Business and the Professions: The Performance Model.* New York: Macmillan, 1988.

Parnell, D. "Will Belly Dancing Be Our Nemesis?" *Community Services Catalyst,* 1982, *12* (3), 4–5.

Queeney, D. S. *Assessing Needs in Continuing Education: An Essential Tool for Quality Improvement.* San Francisco: Jossey-Bass, 1995.

Rippey, R. "Learning from Corporate Education Programs." In L. Curry, J. F. Wergin, and Associates, *Educating Professionals: Responding to New Expectations for Competence and Accountability.* San Francisco: Jossey-Bass, 1993.

JOSEPH N. HANKIN is president of Westchester Community College (New York) and adjunct professor at Teachers College, Columbia University.

Professional associations complement the theoretical education provided by university graduate programs, helping new and aspiring administrators hone practical skills and develop career networks.

The Role of Professional Associations in Developing Academic and Administrative Leaders

Berta Vigil Laden

Graduate programs in higher education administration are most often credited with preparing administrators for leadership positions in academe (Moore, Martorana, and Twombly, 1985), such as the presidency and chief academic and student affairs officers. Yet professional associations and other organizations also play major roles in identifying potential leaders and assisting in their professional development (McDade, 1991; Amey and Twombly, 1992; Twombly, 1995). Using program formats of varying lengths, ranging from short-term workshops to year-long internship experiences, professional associations offer community college faculty and administrators the opportunity to enhance interpersonal and technical competencies, develop strategies for career advancement, and keep up with emerging issues that affect the educational enterprise. Particularly noteworthy are the efforts undertaken by some of these groups to increase the number of women and minority leaders at the mid and upper levels of administration.

The education and training provided by professional associations complement university study in a number of ways. First, they often provide insights into the day-to-day operational problems of administrative life, augmenting the theoretical knowledge offered by university courses. Second, they can help recent graduates adjust to their new administrative roles by helping them to negotiate unfamiliar institutional cultures. Third, they provide new administrators with sponsors or mentors who can build confidence, offer guidance, make introductions, and use their expertise and experiences to assist in the socialization of the newly appointed. Mentors can also help aspiring leaders to map out their short- and long-term goals, and help future leaders to make the most of what they have learned in graduate school.

This chapter reviews some of the efforts undertaken by selected professional organizations to help new and aspiring community college administrators. Some of the programs described here focus on general leadership development that helps both men and women to improve their leadership skills, broaden their network of professional contacts, and increase their opportunities for career advancement. Other programs target women and ethnically diverse individuals, explicitly seeking to increase their numbers in the community college leadership ranks. Examples from both are provided, illustrating the potentially important ways that continuing education offered through professional associations augments university training.

Developing New Leadership

Many professional associations provide assistance for those who aspire to leadership positions at community colleges. These associations help aspiring leaders in at least three ways: by highlighting the formal and informal aspects of educational leadership in the seminars, workshops, and institutes they offer; by enhancing mentoring and network opportunities; and by stressing scholarship as well as the applied and technical skills in the training and preparation of new leaders. A few programs that stress these aspects are described in this section.

American Council on Education Fellows Program. Perhaps one of the best-known leadership programs, the American Council on Education (ACE) Fellows Program offers selected men and women a unique year-long experience in the study of higher education leadership. Each fall, selected faculty and administrators aspiring to senior positions, often the presidency, take a year's leave from their college to assume an internship at another institution. Through a diversified set of experiences, the fellows gain a broader perspective on campus issues by serving as full-time interns to college or university presidents or vice presidents, learning new administrative skills through seminars and practical experiences, talking to national leaders and visiting campuses to develop an understanding of higher education issues in national and regional contexts, and engaging in scholarship that leads to the preparation of a publishable research paper. Besides honing their own skills, the fellows bring new perspectives and information to their home institutions, where they are expected to demonstrate their leadership growth and potential (American Council on Education, 1995). Of particular merit is the program's mentoring component, in which several former ACE fellows work with newly named fellows, often serving as teachers and role models.

In its thirty-one-year history, the ACE Fellows Program has helped over a thousand individuals "gain the experience and perspective necessary to assume significant leadership roles in higher education" (American Council on Education, 1995, p. 1). The highly competitive program particularly prides itself on reaching out to women and ethnic individuals, assisting them to move up the career ladder via the fellowship experience. Also, ACE has made a concerted effort to attract community college applicants, and their applications have increased significantly in recent years. Applicants are nominated by their presidents or chief academic officers with the guarantee that their salaries and benefits will be covered for the full academic year. As part of the rigorous selection process, sixty semifinalists are invited to Washington, D.C. for interviews and thirty are selected as the class for the following academic year.

Due to the high cost of the fellowship experience to home institutions, foundation support for ACE fellows is made available through several different avenues. Noteworthy is a Ford Foundation grant that led to the creation of the ACE Fellows Project for Community Colleges—called Leaders for Tomorrow. Its goals are to increase the participation of community college faculty and administrators, especially women and ethnic individuals, and to foster greater cooperation between community colleges and four-year institutions. These goals are pursued by actively recruiting community college applicants, making available four Ford Foundation grants to defray community college costs, featuring relevant community college topics in seminars throughout the fellows' year, including community college speakers in various program activities, and assisting with the development of fellows' projects that emphasize articulation and collaboration between two- and four-year institutions.

ACE makes concerted efforts to expand the network of professional contacts for fellows and maintain mentoring opportunities following the one-year internship period. The program's alumni group, the Council of Fellows, publishes a newsletter and a directory and also sponsors professional development and social activities at ACE annual meetings. An ACE alumnus who is now president of a California community college notes, "I have found the ACE Fellows' network to be very effective. When I call past ACE Fellows, we usually discuss our experiences in the Fellows Program first and then talk business. When I speak with them, it's like speaking with a friend" (American Council on Education, 1995, p. 14).

Executive Leadership Institute. Established in 1988 by the League for Innovation in the Community College in cooperation with the University of Texas at Austin, the Executive Leadership Institute provides an intensive week-long experience for aspiring presidents who hold senior leadership positions in community colleges and who are interested in and qualified for the presidency by virtue of their educational and experiential backgrounds. While the institute is designed primarily for those who have not yet served in the presidency, new presidents are welcome to apply. Applicants need not be members of the League for Innovation, and international applications are accepted as well.

The institute curriculum helps presidential aspirants answer three basic questions: What is the job? What are my qualifications for the job? How will I do the job? Seminars focus on application and interviewing skills, how to shape and establish the presidency once in the position, relations with trustees and other administrators, and internal and external roles and relations with the college constituency and the public. Other topics include developing and articulating a mission and a vision, working with faculty, assessing student success, dealing with issues of ethics and diversity, collaborating with business and industry in partnership programs, and learning survival techniques and strategies in the role of president (League for Innovation in the Community College, 1996). Institute faculty represent community college leaders in the United States and Canada, experts in leadership development and communications, staff of presidential search organizations, and members of the League for Innovation board of directors. Upon completion of the program, graduates become part of a network of institute alumni (League for Innovation in the Community College, 1996) and meet at various community college functions and conferences, including the annual meeting of the American Association of Community Colleges.

The Presidents' Academy. The Presidents' Academy represents an attempt on the part of the American Association of Community Colleges (AACC) to promote a blend of leadership development and personal renewal for community college leaders (Carrole A. Wolin, personal communication, 1 February 1996). Established in 1975 by the AACC board of directors, the Presidents' Academy offers a five-day opportunity for member presidents to gather in a resort setting to explore issues and topics of interest to community college leaders. The five goals of the academy are to enhance leadership attributes, explore current and emerging issues, network with new and experienced CEOs, exchange ideas and strategies, and rejuvenate, relax, and enjoy the summer experience (American Association of Community Colleges, 1996).

Up to fifty participants, including individuals from outside the United States, are selected annually by the executive committee; gender and ethnic balance is sought in the makeup of the group. Also, both new and senior presidents are encouraged to apply so as to create an enriched forum of sharing, understanding, and revitalizing among participants. Moreover, unlike most other professional development programs, spouses are encouraged to attend and participate in social activities.

The curriculum for each year is based on topics participants express interest in and issues the committee determines are relevant. Topics typically discussed include strategic planning, innovative teaching and learning processes, effects of emerging technology on the learning process, and alternative funding sources. Intercultural and international themes permeate the curriculum as a whole (Carrole A. Wolin, personal communication, February 1, 1996). Unique to the curriculum is the additional emphasis on personal renewal, which is the reason that a relaxed, resortlike setting for the academy is considered important. Using an interactive mode with small groups, participants gather to discuss selected topics in the morning and choose personal activities, including time for reflection, in the afternoon—luxuries not often afforded them back in their institutional settings.

The Leadership Institute. The Consortium for Community College Development (CCCD), consisting of community colleges from twenty-four states and Canada, sponsors an annual three-day Leadership Institute in February under the aegis of the University of Michigan. The Consortium also sponsors several other activities, including a three-day Summer Institute on Institutional Effectiveness and Student Success and a three-day Faculty Development Institute in the fall. As a keystone of CCCD, concepts of leadership are included in the curricula across the various institutes.

The Leadership Institute explores issues that affect community college administration at all levels (president, deans, department chairs, faculty, and staff) and places a particular emphasis on shared governance. The institute offers an opportunity for participants to be "exposed to cutting-edge perspectives" (Einarson, 1995, p. 4) on the fundamental issues and implications of leadership development. Seminar discussions focus on the leader's role in effecting substantive changes and facilitating organizational transformation (Consortium for Community College Development, 1995). According to the CCCD executive director, the seminars help leaders see their multiple functions, which are described as follows: "healers" who "restore trust, heal bruises and wounds, and address past issues"; "bridge builders" who figure out ways to move internally from confrontation to accommodation with the institution's constituents; "community builders" who connect the shared values and purpose of the institution with the larger community; "learners and learning leaders" who focus on the dynamics of the changing world and what is important for the institution; "innovators who rethink, radically redesign, and reinvent the processes of the system"; and finally, "interpreters" who create the climate in which to move forward and promote "a culture of understanding dynamic change and transition" (Carter, 1995, p. 4).

The case study format provides a distinctive backdrop for discussion and shared learning of the issues, dynamics, and processes. Faculty from the University of Michigan and from other institutions provide sessions that link theory with practice through actual case studies based on critical issues relevant to community colleges. Also featured are high-ranking administrators as keynote speakers, interactive sessions with noted practitioners, and informal and recreational activities designed to foster camaraderie and provide networking opportunities. Participants receive a reading list prior to the institute and a bibliography and newsletters afterward so they can continue to expand their knowledge base on leadership issues.

Association of Community College Trustees. The Association of Community College Trustees (ACCT) has two goals for professional development. One is to involve college presidents whenever it can in its activities and workshops, thereby increasing interaction and facilitating team building between presidents and trustees. In an effort to increase the pool of qualified presidential candidates for search committees, the annual convention offers two sessions for potential presidents on applying and interviewing for the presidency. The association extends its interest in community college leadership and the presidency by also providing a CEO search and interim president service for local boards. A bimonthly newsletter and a quarterly journal inform the membership and interested others on current higher education and legislative issues and events.

Another ACCT professional development goal is to foster effective board leadership and responsible, efficient policymaking. At its annual convention, as well as at its regional and state meetings, ACCT offers an array of workshops and activities. According to its stated philosophy, these offerings emphasize the future implications of new and emerging technologies, the future environments community colleges will operate in, changing financial realities, continued attention to performance measures and outcomes assessment, and the challenges all these pose for governance. Finally, to be effective and efficient, ACCT stresses that trustees must learn on the job to do things right while gaining added insight through continuing education (Association of Community College Trustees, 1995).

In that light, ACCT offers an educational program designed to "help develop visionary, caring, competent and responsible lay boards" (Association of Community College Trustees, 1995, p. 1). A multitiered program takes trustees through three levels of preparation, and a certificate is awarded at the conclusion of each level. Trustees select from designated conference activities and workshop sessions offered at the annual, regional, and state ACCT meetings to earn the required twenty-five units to complete each of three levels. Level one emphasizes the nature of trusteeship, community college history and development, governance systems, decision making, and ethics. Level two covers presidential relations, academic policies, employee relations, financial and business policies, assets and facilities, community relations, legal considerations, and political implications. Level three is highly individualized to meet the interests of trustees who wish to further increase their knowledge and skills in leadership, higher education, and community trends and issues.

Promoting Women and Ethnically Diverse Leaders

The low numbers of women and ethnically diverse leaders in community colleges have prompted greater attention to diversity in leadership ranks. Townsend (1995), for example, notes the scarcity of women's voices in the community college at the administrative level. Even in the 1990s, providing community college leadership development for women has remained largely within the purview of a few organizations that receive financial support from various associations and community colleges. The major leadership development opportunities for women are the Summer Institute for Women in Higher Education Administration and the National Institute for Leadership Development. A smaller regional offering is the Asilomar Leadership Skills Seminar in California.

Summer Institute for Women in Higher Education Administration. For twenty-one years, the Summer Institute for Women in Higher Education Administration, cosponsored by Bryn Mawr College and Higher Education Resource Services, Mid-America (HERS, Mid-America), has offered women faculty and administrators intensive training in leadership development. Its specific focus is to improve the status of women in the middle and executive levels of higher education, "areas in which women traditionally have been underrepresented" (Secor, 1995, p. 1). The program's executive director elaborates, "What we really wanted to do [in the mid-1970s] was to increase the numbers straight across the board. There was a pool of talented women who weren't getting key opportunities" (Secor, 1984, p. 3). In response to the perceived need, Secor decided to develop a viable network among women administrators. Thus, the idea of the Summer Institute devoted solely to women and their career interests and concerns emerged.

Since the Summer Institute began in 1976 with initial funding from the William H. Donner Foundation, over fourteen hundred women from the United States, Canada, and African and European countries have participated in the four-week residential program held each year on the Bryn Mawr College campus. While this program does not specifically focus on community colleges, women participants, faculty, and guest speakers are drawn from two- and four-year institutions alike.

The program exposes women working in academia to intensive classroom study, topical seminars, dinners with keynote speakers, and focused dialogues. According to Betsy Metzger (personal communication, 1 November 1995), assistant director of HERS, Mid-America, the four-unit curriculum is revised and fine-tuned annually to be as timely as possible. These units encompass training in management and governance, accounting and budgeting, long-range planning, information technology, decision-making processes, and policy implementation; institutional perspectives on the current pressing issues and problems in higher education with attention to issues of gender and ethnicity; external focus on demographic, political, social, and economic trends, state revenues, tax policies, and accountability; and strategies for professional development with emphasis on women's leadership styles, self-presentation, and career planning. A supportive network of peers and mentors begins at the institute and continues afterward through newsletters and other individual efforts.

The high tuition and travel costs (approximately $6,000 in 1996) pose the biggest obstacle for most women who desire to attend the residential Summer Institute, particularly for community college women (Betsy Metzger, personal communication, 1 November 1995) as staff development funds are limited; thus, most or all of the expenses must be borne by the individual unless other funding sources are found. Metzger found that mailings targeted to community colleges reveal a high interest in attending coupled by an equal concern about the high cost. Some financial assistance by the Bush Foundation and the Evangelical Church of America help participants who are able to piece together funds from various institutional and personal sources as well (Secor, 1995).

The National Institute for Leadership Development. Supported by the American Association for Women in Community Colleges (AAWCC), the Maricopa Community Colleges, Phoenix College, and the League for Innovation in the Community College, the National Institute for Leadership Development

(NILD) is credited with significantly advancing the number of community college women in leadership positions since its founding in 1981 by Mildred Bulpitt and Carolyn Desjardins (Amey and Twombly, 1992; Gillett-Karam, 1994; Twombly, 1995). Recognizing the discrepancy between the large number of women attending community colleges (over 50 percent of the student population) and the small number of women in presidential positions, Bulpitt, a chair of the Phoenix College evening division, decided to take action. Desjardins recalls, "There was a crucial need for a training program and a national network to help women move into major administrative positions. . . . It was important for colleges to respond to the special needs of women and minority students by providing administrators and role models sensitive to those needs" (Desjardins, 1995, p. 2).

Influenced by the works of Gillian (1982) and Belenky, Clinchy, Goldberger, and Tarule (1986), NILD promotes a model of leadership based on inclusiveness, intuition, cooperation, and horizontal connectedness. Emphasis is placed on developing "webs and nets" that are inclusive and collegial and more akin to women's leadership style and preferences than are the hierarchical ladder models (Gillett-Karam, 1994; Twombly, 1995). Desjardins (1995) posits that as women become aware that their styles of leadership are different from men's and equally valuable, they become more comfortable in seeking promotion. Certainly, the statistics collected by the Institute's leaders appear to bear out that belief. In its fourteen-year history, more than three thousand women have attended institute workshops, and of these, seventy have become college presidents while at least nine hundred have advanced to vice presidencies or deanships (Desjardins, 1995).

Under the executive directorship of Desjardins, the leadership program has expanded and now offers six different training opportunities (Desjardins, 1995). *Leaders* is a program for faculty and administrative women who want to assume more responsibility. Seminars focus on building self-esteem and confidence as well as working on a project with a mentor at the home institution. *Leadership II* helps women vice presidents and deans develop greater cooperation between academic and student development faculty and administrators. *Leadership for Change* is for women whose next career step is to become a chief executive officer. Emphasis is on contemporary higher education issues, organizational development, and interviewing and networking skills. *New Issues in Leadership* is for women chief executive officers, giving them an opportunity to discuss professional and personal issues related to the community college presidency.

Kaleidoscope and the *Gender-Based Team Building* seminar are more recent additions that address race and ethnicity and the reality of working with male counterparts as team members within the institution. Kaleidoscope focuses specifically on women administrators of color. The goals of this program are to explore common issues, to provide interaction strategies, to gain greater understanding of ethnic differences and similarities, to strengthen personal leadership styles, to provide role models, and promote team building among diverse groups. The Gender-Based Team Building seminar brings pairs of male and female college representatives together for training. The goals of this seminar are to discuss theory, conditioning, and family-of-origin issues; to develop an understanding of the leadership differences between men and women; and to explore how to use these differences to complement each other's leadership styles. Following the workshop, participants are expected to provide similar training at their own institutions. Finally, participants remain connected through various reunions and seminars throughout the year.

NILD operates out of the Maricopa Community College District in Arizona, but it holds its functions in a variety of locations and in many different formats. Seminars and follow-up events, ranging from several days to a week, are offered in different cities throughout the year. Although attendees come from both two- and four-year institutions, NILD addresses community college issues; its two-year college emphasis is strengthened by the cosponsorship of community college organizations. Costs for attending the seminars vary for each program and exclude transportation, lodging, and meals.

The Asilomar Leadership Skills Seminar for Women on the Move. Moving from the national to the state level, the Asilomar Leadership Skills Seminar for Women on the Move attracts California community college women aspiring to higher-level leadership positions. Women from outside California are also welcome. An intensive five-day seminar is held in January each year at the Asilomar State Conference Center, a seaside resort in the pine and cypress groves between Monterey and Carmel. The seminar's purpose is to provide skills, technical expertise, and networking contacts needed for personal and professional growth to women who have made a commitment to community college administration. The overall expected outcome is that "participants will acquire and successfully accept expanded leadership responsibilities within their own or other California community colleges" (Fisher, 1995, p. 2).

Begun in 1983, the Leadership Skills Seminar is cosponsored by several statewide professional organizations, including the AAWCC, the Association of California Community College Administrators, the Community College League of California, the California Community College Trustees Association, and the Yosemite Community College District. Approximately seven hundred women have participated during its thirteen-year history and have become part of the "network that is creating new leadership for California's community colleges" (Fisher, 1995, p. 2). Women administrators, faculty, staff, and trustees are invited to participate. Topics covered during the seminar include budgeting and finance, campus politics, ethics, career paths, leadership styles, communication skills, staff diversity, student equity, shared governance, and technological change. Presentations and discussions are facilitated by experienced community college leaders, some of whom are former participants who attained positions as chief executive officers.

Pamela Fisher has coordinated the seminar through the Yosemite Community College District from its inception. Fisher also serves as an exemplary role model for participants, having climbed the career ladder from faculty member to district chancellor. Admission to the seminar is competitive, and costs are typically covered by institutional staff development funds. Each year, however, the Marjorie Blaha Memorial Scholarship Fund provides partial payment for two participants who are unable to get full college funding. As part of the application process, applicants are required to secure a letter of recommendation from a senior administrator at their institution as well as a signature of support from the college president. The required institutional recommendations appear to make funding more easily accessible for most women who attend the seminar.

Structuring Continuing Education Programs

The preceding examples illustrate the efforts undertaken by professional associations to foster the skills of community college leaders and assist in the career advancement of individuals, particularly women, who have heretofore been underrepresented in the leadership ranks of community colleges. These efforts provide tomorrow's leaders with informal networking opportunities and practical insights into the culture of institutional administration. Ideally, they help college leaders draw connections between theoretical knowledge gained through university study and practical knowledge gained through experience.

Several conclusions about effective continuing education for community college leaders can be drawn from these illustrations. One is the importance of innovative and thematic efforts that stress the dynamic nature of the community college enterprise. The ACE Fellows Program, with support from the Ford Foundation, is a model of how community college perspectives can be included in leadership development curricula. Other professional organizations in higher education could easily modify their offerings to be more inclusive and representative of diverse institutional settings, including community colleges.

An emphasis on collegial governance and the acknowledgment of formal and informal leadership at all levels of the institution can also be incorporated, as exemplified by the varied institutes offered by the Consortium for Community College Development (CCCD). Presidents cannot provide effective leadership without the collegial support of faculty, staff, students, trustees, alumni, and the greater community. A broadly conceived cooperative, collaborative effort among these constituencies is at the core of the leadership institutes offered by CCCD. It presents an effective paradigm that can be adopted by other professional development programs.

The need to include women and minorities must also be recognized. This is particularly important in light of shifts in national demographics. Attracting women and ethnic individuals as participants in professional development activities is no longer a choice; it is a necessity for all higher education institutions, particularly for community colleges that enroll approximately 40 percent of all college students and nearly 60 percent of students from diverse backgrounds (Cohen and Brawer, 1996). Outreach efforts, such as those used by the ACE Fellows program and the AACC Presidents' Academy, help assure diversity among participants and richer experiences for all.

Efforts to make professional development opportunities more accessible and affordable are also needed. Conference and seminar fees pose a financial hardship for many community college educators who aspire to leadership positions. The cost of attending can be lowered by offering programs in a variety of locations. Short-term workshops and seminars can also increase accessibility and affordability, assisting those individuals who cannot participate in year-long fellowship programs. The NILD seminars are examples, as they are planned in a variety of formats, meet a variety of needs (depending on where individuals are on the career ladder), are conducted in different locations, and offered at differing levels of cost. Sponsoring organizations and associations can seek ways to provide full and partial assistance for those who may feel excluded from participation due to lack of adequate institutional resources. Foundations, alumni, and business and industry, as well as community colleges themselves, are all potential sources of funds. Again, the ACE Fellows Program provides an example of how professional organizations can tap various funding sources.

Finally, associations can use a variety of media to inform educational leaders about the various professional development activities they offer. An important and growing resource is electronic technology, which can be used to inform, advertise, and accept applications from potential institute and seminar attendees. Moreover, use of electronic technology is ideal for disseminating newsletters, networking with larger groups through list servers, and announcing new positions and upcoming events, to name but a few possibilities.

Conclusions

Gone are the days of taking a new position after completion of a doctoral degree and learning the necessary skills on the job. Productive, articulate, responsive leadership is expected as soon as new administrators assume office. Although higher education graduate programs offer theoretical grounding, leadership perspectives, and the academic credentials needed by aspiring leaders, they often do not provide the hands-on skills needed by educational decision makers. Moreover, many graduates also lack the network of connections necessary to enter the job market and promote their careers. The opportunity to gain practical and conceptual orientations, improve interpersonal skills, learn the latest management and technological skills, develop network alliances, and keep abreast of changes has led to more training opportunities being developed as part of annual association meetings and membership offerings. With an increased interest in these activities from members and non-members alike due to the perceived benefits of attending such events, professional associations have stepped in to address the growing demand for leadership training.

References

American Association of Community Colleges. *AACC Professional Development: AACC Presidents' Academy*. Washington, D.C.: American Association of Community Colleges, 1996.

American Council on Education. *1995–96 ACE Fellows Program*. Washington, D.C.: American Council on Education, 1995.

Amey, M. J., and Twombly, S. B. "Re-visioning Leadership in Community Colleges." *Review of Higher Education,* 1992, *15* (2), 125–150.

Association of Community College Trustees. *Trustee Education Recognition Program Guide*. Washington, D.C.: Association of Community College Trustees, 1995.

Belenky, M. F., Clinchy, B. M., Goldberger, N. R., and Tarule, J. M. *Women's Ways of Knowing*. New York: Basic Books, 1986.

Carter, P. "Redefining Leadership Roles." *Capsule,* 1995, *8* (1), 4.

Cohen, A. M., and Brawer, F. B. *The American Community College*. (3rd ed.) San Francisco: Jossey-Bass, 1996.

Consortium for Community College Development. *Capsule,* 1995, *8* (1), 1–6.

Desjardins, C. *National Institute for Leadership Development Handbook*. Phoenix, Ariz.: National Institute for Leadership Development, 1995.

Einarson, M. "Join Us in Tacoma." *Capsule,* 1995, *8* (1), 1.

Fisher, P. *Asilomar Leadership Skills Seminar for Women on the Move: Handbook*. Modesto, Calif.: Yosemite Community College District, 1995.

Gillian, C. *In a Different Voice: Psychological Theory and Women's Development*. Cambridge, Mass.: Harvard University Press, 1982.

Gillett-Karam, R. "Women and Leadership." In G. A. Baker III (ed.), *A Handbook on the Community College in America*. Westport, Conn.: Greenwood Press, 1994.

League for Innovation in the Community College. *The League for Innovation in the Community College: 1996 Leadership Institute*. Mission Viejo, Calif.: League for Innovation in the Community College, 1996.

McDade, S. K. "New Pathways in Leadership and Professional Development." In J. D. Fife and L. F. Goodchild (eds.), *Administration as a Profession*. New Directions for Higher Education, no. 76. San Francisco: Jossey-Bass, 1991.

Moore, K. M., Martorana, S. V., and Twombly, S. *Today's Academy Leaders: A National Study of Administrators in Community Colleges*. University Park: Center for the Study of Higher Education, Pennsylvania State University, 1985.

Secor, C. "Preparing the Individual for Institutional Leadership: The Summer Institute." In A. Tinsley, C. Secor, and S. Kaplan (eds.), *Women in Higher Education Administration.* New Directions for Higher Education, no 45. San Francisco: Jossey-Bass, 1984.

Secor, C. *Summer Institute for Women in Higher Education: Handbook*. Denver: Higher Education Resource Services, Mid-America, 1995.

Townsend, B. K. "Editor's Notes." In B. K. Townsend (ed.), *Gender and Power in the Community College*. New Directions for Community Colleges, no. 89. San Francisco: Jossey-Bass, 1995.

Twombly, S. B. "Gendered Images of Community College Leadership: What Messages They Send." In B. K. Townsend (ed.), *Gender and Power in the Community College*. New Directions for Community Colleges, no. 89. San Francisco: Jossey-Bass, 1995.

BERTA VIGIL LADEN is assistant professor of higher education at Vanderbilt University, Nashville, Tennessee.

Community college administration faculty affect future leadership in the community college by determining which students are admitted, what they are taught, who teaches them, and how they are treated.

The Role of the Professoriate in Influencing Future Community College Leadership

Barbara K. Townsend

A doctorate in higher education or community college administration has served numerous individuals as a passport to senior administrative positions in the community college. Moore, Martorana, and Twombly (1985) examined the backgrounds and career paths of more than 1,500 two-year college administrators and discovered that over 35 percent of the 675 administrators with first doctoral degrees had a degree in higher education administration. This group included approximately 41 percent of the presidents, over 39 percent of the chief student affairs officers, and over 34 percent of the chief academic affairs officers in the study.

Not only do many current two-year college senior administrators possess a doctorate in higher education or community college administration, many future administrators are also likely to have one. To determine the value of a doctorate in higher education administration for senior administrative positions, Townsend and Wiese (1990, 1992) asked a national sample of two- and four-year senior administrators their perceptions of the degree. The researchers found that a doctorate in higher education was most accepted in the two-year sector (1992). Over 80 percent of two-year college respondents perceived a doctorate in higher education as at least comparable to a degree in an academic discipline for individuals applying for a student affairs administrative position, an institutional management position, or a college presidency. More than

---

A version of this chapter was published previously in *Community College Week,* July 3, 1995, pp. 4–5.

60 percent saw a higher education doctorate as at least comparable to one from an academic discipline for applicants for academic affairs positions (1990).

Given how well accepted the higher education or community college administration doctorate is in the two-year sector, faculty in higher education or community college administration programs play a major role in determining who the next generation of community college leaders will be and what they will be like. From a structural perspective, faculty in these programs serve as gatekeepers: they have the authority to admit certain individuals to doctoral study and to deny admission to others. Individuals admitted to study can then earn the credential necessary to move into senior-level administrative positions. Individuals without this credential hit a "paper ceiling." By determining who will be accepted into their programs and who will graduate, faculty in community college administration programs thus have a tremendous influence on the future leadership of the community college.

Faculty also influence future community college leadership in other ways. Once through the gate of program admission, students are influenced by their doctoral experiences. They are influenced by what curriculum they are taught, who teaches them, and how they are treated as students. In this chapter, I will detail the role faculty in community college administration programs do play and can play in influencing the future leadership of community colleges.

Who Is Admitted

Community colleges enjoy the most diverse student body in higher education. Those who will lead the community college need to reflect, understand, and appreciate this diversity. Decisions about who is admitted into community college administration doctoral programs affect the demographic diversity of future community college leadership. If women and minorities are not admitted into these programs, then most future leaders of community colleges are not likely to be women and people of color.

Graduation rates from higher education and community college administration programs suggest that the programs have become very inclusive of women students but less so of minority students. In 1987, almost 60 percent of those who received a doctorate in higher education were female, as compared to about 13 percent in 1972 (Townsend and Mason, 1990). The percentage of minority graduates from these programs is much lower. In 1987, approximately 17 percent were minorities (Townsend and Mason, 1990).

A few community college administration programs present a student body far more diversified than the national profile. The community college administration program at the University of Texas at Austin, under the leadership of John Roueche, has been highly successful in recruiting and retaining minorities and women. Since Roueche assumed the leadership of the program in 1970, over 50 percent of the students in each class or cohort group have been women and minorities (Rodriguez, 1993). This program stands as a model of ways to attract and graduate a diverse student body.

What Curriculum Is Taught

Gender, racial, and ethnic diversity in the student body is important, but it is not sufficient to develop an understanding and appreciation of cultural diversity in future community college leaders. Faculty in community college administration programs need to provide a curriculum that reflects new scholarship about women and minorities.

First of all, the curriculum in community college administration programs needs to reflect new models of leadership, not just the traditional models designed by and for white males. Amey and Twombly (1992) and Twombly (1995) have led the way in critiquing the typical language and models of community college leadership. They have demonstrated how the language and models are gendered in ways that work against the likelihood of women being viewed as leaders. Twombly (1995) has also noted that these same models preclude minorities from being seen as likely leaders of community colleges. Professors in community college administration programs must reexamine the research and the models of leadership they present and be sensitive to any cultural biases in them.

The curriculum must also reflect an awareness and acknowledgment that race, ethnicity, gender, and social class affect individuals' experiences and perceptions, as well as those of community college leaders. Bowen (1993), president of LaGuardia Community College, expresses this point well when he writes about his experiences as a community college president. He maintains that as an African American, his perspective on pluralism and inclusiveness is different than that of a member of the dominant culture. He states, "It is one thing to employ rhetoric to preach inclusiveness but an entirely different matter to make it come alive through persuasive examples that emerge from our unique experiences" (p. 7).

Students also need to learn that cultural and gender differences affect the dynamics of administrative teams (Burgos-Sasscer, 1993; Fernandez, 1991). Current and future leaders need to be sensitized to the need to develop "new management models and leadership styles" that will "capitalize on and nurture diversity" (Burgos-Sasscer, 1993, p. 89). For example, some research indicates that women, people of color, and those from a working-class background prefer a collaborative mode of management rather than the individualistic one emphasized in bureaucratic approaches to governance (Fernandez, 1991; Cannon, 1994). These new management models and leadership styles should be taught in community college administration programs.

The professoriate in community college administration programs needs to address gender and cultural differences in leadership styles—and not just by offering a token class meeting or two on women and minority students or women and minorities in administration. Rather, attention to cultural differences needs to be paid continually and systematically whenever relevant.

Discussions about the intersection of gender, race, and class can be disconcerting, difficult, and uncomfortable for many people. Cannon (1994) provides some excellent ground rules for class discussions about how race, class, gender, and other factors affect power and privilege in society. Using her guidelines will enable professors to facilitate these discussions, which must take place if we are honest about issues facing community college leaders. For example, one ground rule is that class members can request that comments made in class are not to be repeated outside of class. These requests for confidentiality are to be honored so that students will feel safe in expressing their opinions about provocative issues.

Curriculum is more than content; it is also process, or how the content is taught (Toombs and Tierney, 1991). No matter what the content of a course, if it is taught via the traditional lecture or banking model of education, then the message to students is that they have little or nothing to contribute. In the *banking model* of education, faculty possess knowledge that they deposit into their students' supposedly empty heads (Freire, 1970). The students' role is a passive one of absorbing and later regurgitating on examinations what they have memorized of the professor's lecture. The implicit message is that their experiences have limited value in doctoral courses. The banking model also represents a top-down approach to the teaching-learning process and thus an implicit model of leadership that is antithetical to current models of leadership such as Total Quality Management and Continuous Quality Improvement.

One alternative approach is that known as the *midwife model* of teaching (Belenky, Clinchy, Goldberger, and Tarule, 1990). In this approach the teacher serves as midwife to help students give birth to their own ideas about a subject. Teachers using this approach view students as possessing tacit knowledge that needs to be drawn out and articulated. Furthermore, "the student is treated from the start not as subordinate or as object but as 'independent, a subject'" (p. 316). Given that so many of the students in community college administration programs are mature adults in responsible professional positions, this model seems more appropriate than the banking model.

Who Teaches in Community College Administration Programs

Students' perceptions of the curriculum are affected not only by what and how they are taught but also by who does the teaching. This is one of the premises behind affirmative action in the hiring of faculty. Currently the professoriate in higher education doctoral programs is not very diverse. Nelson's (1991) study indicated that in 1989 22 percent of higher education program faculty were female. Newell and Kuh (1989) found that in 1986 less than 7 percent of higher education faculty were people of color: 4.4 percent blacks and 2.2 percent Hispanics.

The opportunity to diversify the professoriate in community college administration programs lies ahead. Almost 60 percent of faculty in higher education doctoral programs were over fifty in 1989. Consequently there will be ample opportunity in ten to fifteen years for hiring a new generation of professors in these programs (Nelson, 1991). We need to use this opportunity to hire faculty that represent diverse groups and alternative perspectives.

Sometimes efforts are made to diversify faculty in community college administration programs by hiring women and minorities as part-time faculty.

A problem with this solution is that part-time faculty are peripheral within the academy by virtue of working part time. Putting women and people of color primarily in part-time positions only serves to marginalize these groups further. It may also send a message that they are not good enough to be hired as full-time faculty, only as part-time faculty. University administrators and full-time faculty need to guard against considering this practice as a sufficient means for diversifying the faculty in community college administration programs.

How Students Are Treated

Program faculty determine the formal curriculum, defined as the knowledge, skills, and beliefs that are consciously, deliberately taught in the classroom. However, the formal curriculum is not the only mode by which students come to understand the meaning of a profession such as higher education adminis-tration. Rather, "the meanings that people develop within professional pro-grams are the product of constant interaction, conflict, and interpretation" (Rhoades, 1991, p. 368).

Faculty need to realize that what they do in their courses and programs reverberates in ways they may never understand. How faculty treat students gets construed by students in ways that faculty may never intend but that may work to undermine the lessons taught in the formal curriculum. For example, the for-mal curriculum may include espousal of the Total Quality Management approach to leadership, whereby the opinions of all organizational constituents are sought and valued. If students are not routinely asked what they think about the over-all curriculum, the content of specific courses, and faculty's teaching abilities and if their comments are not then considered in decisions about the curriculum and faculty, then professors are sending mixed messages. In this instance, the for-mal curriculum delivers the message that all constituencies' perspectives are valuable and need to be considered. The hidden curriculum, as demonstrated by the failure to ask for or consider the input of students about teaching and curriculum, delivers quite another message: "Do as we say, not as we do."

Another example of a possible hidden curriculum involves which students get asked to work with faculty on research projects and presentations. If fac-ulty only choose to work with those like them, that is, if white, male faculty only ask white, male students to work with them, then nonwhite and female students learn quickly that any messages in the formal curriculum about the necessity for inclusion are empty words.

Conclusion

Regardless of their own gender, race or ethnicity, or social-class background, the professoriate in community college administration programs must model inclusive perspectives in their recruitment and admissions, curricular choices, selection of program faculty, and treatment of students. By so doing, they will fulfill the responsibilities inherent in their role as gatekeepers to leadership positions in the community college. They will also help the next generation of community college leaders to reflect what the community college is: inclusive, democratic, and egalitarian.

References

Amey, M. J., and Twombly, S. B. "Re-visioning Leadership in Community Colleges." *Review of Higher Education,* 1992, *15* (2), 125–150.

Belenky, M. F., Clinchy, B. M., Goldberger, N. R., and Tarule, J. M. "Connected Teaching." In C. F. Conrad and J. G. Haworth, *Curriculum in Transition.* ASHE Readers Series. New York: Ginn Press, 1990.

Bowen, R. C. "Vision and the Black Community College President." Speech at La Guardia Community College, Long Island City, N.Y., May 1993.

Burgos-Sasscer, R. "New Players in Management." In R. L. Alfred and P. Carter (eds.), *Changing Managerial Imperatives.* New Directions for Community Colleges, no. 84. San Francisco: Jossey-Bass, 1993.

Cannon, L. W. "Fostering Positive Race, Class, and Gender Dynamics in the Classroom." In K. Feldman and M. Paulsen (eds.), *Teaching and Learning in the College Classroom.* ASHE Reader Series. New York: Ginn Press, 1994.

Fernandez, J. P. *Managing a Diverse Work Force.* Lexington, Mass.: Heath, 1991.

Freire, P. *Pedagogy of the Oppressed.* New York: Seabury Press, 1970.

Moore, K. M., Martorana, S. V., and Twombly, S. *Today's Academy Leaders: A National Study of Administrators in Community Colleges.* University Park: Center for the Study of Higher Education, Pennsylvania State University, 1985.

Nelson, G. "Higher Education Doctoral Programs: A Demographic Portrait." In J. D. Fife and L. F. Goodchild (eds.), *Administration as a Profession.* New Directions for Higher Education, no. 76. San Francisco: Jossey-Bass, 1991.

Newell, L. J., and Kuh, G. "Taking Stock: The Higher Education Professoriate." *Review of Higher Education,* 1989, *13* (1), 63–90.

Rhoades, G. "Professional Education: Stratifying Curricula and Perpetuating Privilege in Higher Education." In J. Smart (ed.), *Higher Education: Handbook of Theory and Research,* Vol. 7. New York: Agathon Press, 1991.

Rodriguez, R. "University of Texas at Austin Leads the Way with Its Community College Graduate Program." *Black Issues in Higher Education,* 1993, *10* (10), 43–46.

Toombs, W., and Tierney, W. G. *Meeting the Mandate: Renewing the College and Departmental Curriculum.* ASHE-ERIC Higher Education Series, no. 6. Washington, D.C.: George Washington University, 1991.

Townsend, B. K., and Mason, S. O. "Career Paths of Graduates of Higher Education Doctoral Programs." *Review of Higher Education,* 1990, *14* (1), 63–81.

Townsend, B. K., and Wiese, M. "Value of the Higher Education Doctorate For Community College Administrators." *Community/Junior College Quarterly of Research and Practice,* 1990, *14* (4), 337–347.

Townsend, B. K., and Wiese, M. "The Value of a Doctorate in Higher Education for Student Affairs Administrators." *NASPA Journal,* 1992, *30* (1), 51–58.

Twombly, S. B. "Gendered Images of Community College Leadership: What Messages They Send." In B. K. Townsend (ed.), *Gender and Power in the Community College.* New Directions for Community Colleges, no. 89. San Francisco: Jossey-Bass, 1995.

BARBARA K. TOWNSEND is professor of higher education and coordinator of the higher and adult education program in the Department of Leadership at the University of Memphis. She is also a former community college faculty member and administrator.

Graduate courses can help students understand democratic models of leadership, which recognize the leadership potential of all faculty and staff, not simply the college president.

Diversity, Discourse, and Democracy: Needed Attributes in the Next Generation of Community College Leadership Programs

Barbara S. Gibson-Benninger, James L. Ratcliff, Robert A. Rhoads

A fundamental challenge facing community college leaders is to create an environment in which the diverse qualities and abilities of students and staff make positive contributions to the growth and development of the organization. Creating such environments involves viewing the organization as a culture and enacting strategies that empower people to participate in decision making and change. When an organization is viewed as a culture, leadership is not limited to those in a few top administrative positions within a hierarchical structure. When viewed as a relational process, leadership moves beyond the leader-follower dichotomy that reduces and constrains visions of organizational change. The democratic community college may be shaped by all the organization members and the dynamic social context in which they operate. Therefore, a strong organization is one that provides opportunities for a wide range of members to assert themselves as purveyors of organizational direction. Similarly, viewing leadership as a dialogic, relational process wherein all interested actors are engaged in shaping the future helps empower individuals, harness the latent potential and tension that diversity brings to the college, and avail the organization of the full talent of the people associated with it.

This chapter examines how community college graduate programs might be reframed around democratic views of leadership based on a cultural model of organizations and a relational model of discourse and communication. In embracing the ideals of democracy, our thinking reflects the work of John Dewey (1916). For Dewey, democracy was a way of envisioning social life such that all people have the opportunity to contribute to important decisions shaping their lives. Such decisions, however, are not made selfishly but are rooted in a larger concern for others. As Dewey noted, "Democracy is more than a form of government; it is primarily a mode of associated living, of conjoint communicated experience. [It is] the extension in space of the number of individuals who participate in an interest so that each has to refer his own action to that of others, and to consider the action of others to give point and direction to his own" (p. 93).

Democratic Leadership

Democratic leadership, we suggest, calls for a recognition that differences are not always best reconciled, that consensus is not always the aim of organizations, and that the tension between perspectives within an organizational culture may be the dynamic that propels the organization in new and creative directions. Writing in 1962, Goodman criticized modern management for its intention to "enforce a false harmony in a situation that should be rife with conflict" (p. 8). It is the modernist emphasis on harmony and commonality inherent in traditional treatments of organizations that democratic forms of leadership seek to escape. Such an endeavor rests with the ability and willingness of individuals to enter into ongoing dialogue in which the ideal of community is reflected by the commitment to understanding diversity and difference. Thus, a close understanding of the nature of dialogue, discourse, and diversity—and the style of communication they foster—is essential to democratic leadership.

A democratic vision of leadership as dialogic and relational moves away from traditional views predominantly framed by the *Great Man* theory, which holds that individuals are primary and direct causes of historical events. This view tends "to give insufficient weight to the role institutions play in forming the ideas of leaders, in structuring the problems they faced, and in molding the solutions they might attempt and achieve" (Shafer, 1974, p. 31). Research on college establishment and founding attributed the development of early junior colleges to great men such as William Rainey Harper at the University of Chicago, Alexis Lange at the University of California, and Henry Tappan at the University of Michigan (Gleazer, 1968; Goodwin, 1971). Because these persons were university presidents, leadership was defined in terms of the actions of a few heroic men in the office of the presidency, particularly the presidency of senior institutions (Ratcliff, 1987a, 1987b; Amey and Twombly, 1992). This research failed to yield information on the complex of social, political, and economic relationships existing between college and community.

Studies of organizational change stress the role of innovators—individuals who may hold little formal power, but become knowledgeable champions for certain innovations, and evidence a willingness to try out new ideas, practices, or technology. Similarly, organizational change literature points to opinion leaders (again, often people without formal authority, but nonetheless influential in the organization) in rallying support for reform, renewal, or transformation. Group processes, relational dynamics, and interpersonal interactions also have significant bearing on how organizations move (or fail to move) toward change (Baldridge, 1971; Lindquist, 1978; Morgan, 1986; Rogers and Rogers, 1976). Tomorrow's community college leaders will not simply reside in the president's office and they cannot survive on visions alone; they must understand the complexities of the college's rapidly changing organizational culture and multicultural social context.

A democratic view of leadership resists the individualist temptations of the Great Man theory and suggests instead that leaders must involve others in collaborative processes. Such a view of leadership challenges leaders to develop a complex understanding of the organization and how members create meaning in the organizational setting. Recent research on colleges and universities highlights how viewing them as cultures is helpful in understanding the complex webs of meaning inherent in organizational life (Bensimon, 1990; Rhoads and Valadez, 1996; Rhoads and Tierney, 1992; Tierney, 1993). We find the organizational culture perspective to be compatible with democratic principles in that cultural understanding enables organization leaders to more closely examine the multiple others with whom leaders must interact and ultimately form a collective vision. The fact that multiple others exist within organizational settings calls attention to the multicultural quality that has become a defining point of U.S. society. In what follows, we discuss some of these issues in greater detail before delineating their implications for community college leadership programs.

Organizational Culture and Change

To understand the vision of community college leadership suggested in this chapter, we argue that it is helpful to view organizations as cultures. As Bensimon (1990) notes: "To view the institution as a cultural entity is to see it as a system of shared meanings, maintained by symbolic processes" (p. 77). Seen in this light, "Organizational culture is the glue that holds the institution together" (Rhoads and Tierney, 1992, p. 5). An emphasis on culture as a means to make sense of organizational life is often referred to as the cultural perspective or as a "cultural frame" (Bolman and Deal, 1991). Cultural perspectives of higher education have become a popular tool for understanding college and university organizational life (Chaffee and Tierney, 1988; Clark, 1972, 1987; Kuh and Whitt, 1988; Tierney, 1988).

From a cultural perspective, organization members who have leadership responsibilities must come to terms with various aspects of the organization's culture. For example, understanding an institution's history and traditions may be vital to correctly interpreting contemporary behaviors of students or faculty. Traditions and organizational sagas shape and constrain change within any institution of higher education (Clark, 1972), and are the stuff of its history (Shafer, 1974). A cultural perspective challenges leaders to be aware of the symbolic aspects of campus life, such as the significance of rituals and cere-monies that often convey deep meanings to those involved. The values and beliefs organization members hold also are part of the fabric that we call cul-ture and must be understood by leaders. A cultural perspective also has impli-cations for how organizational change is conceptualized.

Leaders assume special, often ad hoc, roles within cultures. Negotiation of diverse views, interests, and needs within a system of shared meaning becomes critical to progress and change. Similar negotiation between internal and exter-nal constituencies, communities, and stakeholders is also necessary. Often such negotiation has been seen as a process of bringing compliance to previously established or presidentially proclaimed college mission and goals. Differences within the community college are to be resolved, minimized, or neutralized through consensus development, compliance, or coercion processes. Such a perspective on leadership views the absence of tension as a precondition to progress. It may be less arduous for a leader to subsume differences and diver-sity within the organization, but it limits the extent to which the leader will tap the talent within the organization. We urge a conceptualization of change that is not based on leader-follower dichotomies and that has as its foundation the relational nature of human action within organizations (Baxter and Mont-gomery, 1996; Montgomery, 1995).

From the usual leader-follower dichotomy, an objective of leadership is to resolve differences and to resolve or minimize conflict within the college. The leader performs a similar function between the college and society. It is ironic that viewed from the leader-follower paradigm, the absence of tension is the basis for change. We offer as an alternative a relational, democratic view that sees alternate perspectives, experience, and interests as representing tensions that instigate change and propel the college community to explore new direc-tions. Contradiction and conflict are normal facets of an organizational culture, and are essential characteristics of the change process in the engaged, democ-ratic college community. The role of change agent is transformed from one of resolving differences, seeking compromise, and minimizing conflict to one of acknowledging and examining differences and embracing diversity as the basis of empowerment, enterprise, ingenuity, and change.

The role of change agent is a vital responsibility of organization members assigned to key roles in a community college. From a cultural perspective, introducing change involves confronting values, beliefs, and norms held by various members. This means that for change to take root, leaders must rec-ognize the cultural elements (attitudes, values, beliefs, norms, and so on) that will be most affected by change. Since these cultural elements are fundamen-tal to how organizational life is constructed, leaders must recognize that change has a deeply felt impact on members.

When we think of organizations as cultures—as systems of shared mean-ing—it is easier to understand how organizational change ought to involve collaborative processes. Although high-ranking administrators may be able to impose structural changes, such as adding new positions, eliminating programs, combining units, or forming new committees, such actions also involve altering shared understandings across the college, and therefore take more than executive fiat to accomplish. Instead, for change to take root, members must envision the organization, their role within the organization, and the role of others in a new and perhaps innovative manner. If a change in sense-making strategies does not occur, then change is unlikely to take root and a new idea becomes nothing more than a tumbleweed rolling across the organizational terrain.

Because a fundamental change in the way members make sense of organizational life is needed, involving them at the early stages of any change effort is essential to success. This means that change efforts ought to be based on democratic processes that involve a wide range of organization members and tap the leadership abilities of diverse campus constituents. Creating opportunities for a broad array of campus voices to be heard also is compatible with emerging views of multiculturalism—issues community colleges have been slow to address (Rhoads and Valadez, 1996).

Diversity, Democracy, and Discourse

Multiculturalism involves more than merely including diverse peoples within educational settings; multiculturalism also poses a challenge to how we structure those educational settings and the opportunities we create for organization members to participate in decision making. As Bensimon (1994) maintains: "We must recognize that the perspective of multiculturalism, the struggle to create a more democratic, pluralistic education system in this country, is part of the struggle to empower people" (p. 7).

In terms of how college and university leadership ought to be conceptualized, democratic strategies are obviously more conducive to empowering diverse constituents. This is especially true of community colleges, where nearly half of the students are from underrepresented groups. If they are to truly embrace multiculturalism, community colleges must create opportunities for diverse perspectives to shape the fabric of the organization.

What we suggest here is that community colleges are not only to be democratizing agents in terms of their contributions to the social mobility of culturally diverse students; just as important, community colleges must be democratic educational centers. The perspective we put forth is that community college leaders ought to be guided by a commitment to democratic principles such as inclusiveness and equal opportunity for all. Although prior community college literature advocated participatory forms of leadership (for example, Richardson, Blocker, and Bender, 1972), we argue that specific attention needs to be given to building leadership and community around cultural diversity and the inclusion of diverse peoples and their perspectives. This is the essence of Tierney's (1993) vision of colleges and universities as "communities of difference." The process of leadership in this sort of community will be dialogic and relational rather than consensual (Baxter and Montgomery, 1996; Montgomery, 1995).

A democratic view of leadership means involving a range of voices in debates and discussions about the mission and identity of the college itself. We are not suggesting that the decision-making capability of community college presidents and other senior administrators be shackled. What we are suggesting, however, is that over the long haul, the mission and identity of the college need to be deeply rooted within the culture of the organization. This necessitates involving diverse faculty, staff, students, and community members in a more collaborative process.

Leadership envisioned as the practice of democracy situates the capacity to influence the direction and identity of the institution in all organization members. This is contrary to popular conceptions of community college leadership, which tend to situate power and influence in the presidency. For example, Roueche, Baker, and Rose (1989) discuss the importance of a shared sense of vision based on understanding organizational culture, but they limit their discussion of leadership to the role of the president. Their conception of leadership suggests that other organization members have little influence over the vision and direction of the community college. Likewise, Vaughan (1989) equates the community college presidency with leadership, as if all presidents are "leaders," when arguably leadership oftentimes is situational and context-specific (Bensimon, Neumann, and Birnbaum, 1989). Roueche, Baker, and Rose (1989) see leaders as individuals with a vision and a capacity to mobilize teams to put that vision in effect on campus. Although teamwork is discussed, the vision nonetheless comes directly from the president. Again, studies of organizational change affirm the role of the informal innovator and opinion leader, as well as the individuals with assigned formal power (such as the president) in reform, renewal and transformation (Havelock and others, 1971; Lindquist, 1978; Morgan, 1986; Rogers and Rogers, 1976).

A commitment to democracy means that community colleges must strive to create leadership opportunities for women and underrepresented minorities. A student population of women, older students, or students of color does not ensure a multicultural campus; even though the student body manifests the demographic characteristics of the larger community or society, the presence of individuals from various groups does not ensure their participation in organizational decision making. Clearly, women and minorities have been grossly underrepresented in leadership roles at colleges and universities (Fulton, 1984). One reason underrepresented groups may not move into administrative positions is the lack of people from those groups currently in positions of power and authority. "Mentors have traditionally been white males who have not surprisingly selected white men as protegees" (Schneider, 1991, p. 4). Gillett-Karam, Roueche, and Roueche (1991) call this the "concept of reproduction of self" where the person leaving the position hires someone to replace himself, and therefore believes that person should be like himself (p. 30). Mentoring is a form of leadership dialogue and relational communication that is not instinctively employed by persons in positions of responsibility within an organization; it needs understanding, targeted educational development, and practice.

The lack of mentors is obviously one barrier to increasing the leadership roles of women and underrepresented minorities. Lack of mentoring also contributes to feelings of isolation as well as exclusion from informal networks. In a survey of women community college administrators, Capozzoloi (1989) found that, "Having mentors may be the single most important factor in an administrator's career development" (p. 7). And Schneider (1991) found mentoring to differ significantly along gender lines, with women remaining in readiness-to-advance phases longer due to the lack of assurance to move on to the next career phase. Our lack of attention to discourse, diversity, and democracy in leadership has made mentoring across gender or ethnic lines problematic, but such skills can be developed (Gergen, 1995).

Another factor believed to contribute to the challenge of hiring faculty and staff from underrepresented groups is the so-called *dry pipeline*—a lack of women and minority applicants available and applying for positions (Parsons, 1992, p. 6). This is a particular concern of rural community colleges, where the diversity of the local community is often limited. What is clear, however, is that multiculturalism calls attention to the fact that mere recognition that women and minorities are underrepresented is not enough; a commitment to multiculturalism involves hiring qualified underrepresented faculty and staff despite the challenges.

Diversity can be a powerful force when used as a basis for relational discourse and empowerment to create truly democratic community colleges for the future. However, the predominant paradigm—the leader-follower formula—tends to view and treat diversity as a set of isolated human relations problems to be solved or as a group of outside mandates, quotas, and political pressures to be met (Bensimon, 1994; Gibson-Benninger and Ratcliff, 1996). Ways to eliminate the problem of the dry pipeline include recruitment of dual-career couples, expanding the search in national advertisements, including minority representatives from the community on search committees, and calling upon women and minorities employed by the institution to recruit. The ability to engage across campus, tapping into its diversity of talent, is a premium ability to effect democratic leadership.

Community college education was meant to be egalitarian. It was designated by the Truman Commission as a harbinger of democratization with opportunities for all, but it may strive to achieve this for its students while overlooking these principles when hiring new employees. Most educators agree that new leadership is needed. Leadership has for many years been seen from a traditional model (Gillett-Karam, Roueche, and Roueche, 1991) based on a masculine paradigm of leadership that values and rewards aggression, independence, and autonomy. The leadership styles of women and minorities may offer alternative perspectives and add much to a democratic community college of the future. Tapping the imagination of innovators, opinion leaders, and campus communities broadens the pool of talent, energy, and ideas within the organization.

Such skills of engagement go far beyond the traditional management notions of delegation to the ability to create meaningful and sustained discourse.

Community colleges committed to principles of democracy must work to create opportunities for diverse groups. Graduate programs in higher education can play a key role in how future community college leaders are prepared and the role that they might play in creating more democratic settings.

Implications for Graduate Programs in Community College Leadership

Based on the vision of democratic leadership described throughout this chapter, we offer the following points as a general framework for rethinking how community college graduate programs might be structured.

Understand organizations as cultures. Future community college leaders need to have a deep understanding of today's complex organizations. A cultural perspective is one organizational framework that encourages the depth of understanding needed to comprehend the multiple constituents and meanings undergirding today's community colleges. Understanding the culture of the college helps to clarify the symbolic dimensions of organizational life and provides essential understanding for creating organizational change. Graduate programs for community college personnel need to make sure that organizational theory in general and cultural perspectives in particular are given extensive treatment within the curriculum. This can be accomplished by a comprehensive course on organizational theory, the examination of institutions where multiculturalism has been successfully implemented, and by hearing current community college leaders discuss the ways they accomplish the successful integration of cultural perspectives at their institutions.

Recognize the importance of multiculturalism. Future community college leaders need to have a multicultural understanding of today's world. This involves developing sensitivity to the different sense-making strategies and decision-making styles of diverse constituents. It also means coming to terms with the ways in which race, ethnicity, gender, sexual orientation, age, and other psychologically salient characteristics shape human experience and identity. Inclusion of a multicultural emphasis ought to occur in two ways. First, a course on multiculturalism and related issues may be offered. Second, graduate programs should also seek to ensure that multiculturalism cuts across the curriculum by including various multicultural topics in all courses. For example, a course on administration could suggest ways in which searches might be conducted to foster greater diversity. Courses focused on college students could devote significant time to student identity issues and the role culture plays in shaping students' experiences.

Embrace democratic practices across graduate programs. The idea of democracy discussed by Dewey extends throughout all phases of life. If we desire future community college leaders to embrace democratic principles, then the experiences we develop as part of graduate preparation ought to reflect these same values. This means that the practices of graduate programs, including the pedagogical styles and strategies that teachers enact, ought to reflect democratic ideals such as greater inclusion and participation. In practice, this means involving graduate students to a greater degree in departmental decision making and creating classroom environments where all students have the opportunity to participate. Team building through cooperative and collaborative work is one way to encourage greater classroom participation.

Understand the difference between compliance and empowerment. To be effective leaders, community college administrators, faculty, and staff need to understand the importance of discourse and group dynamics. The leader-follower paradigm emphasizes centralized plans and strategies situated with individuals at the top of the organization. This view presumes that the highest levels of wisdom and insight about the health and future of the organization reside at the top. By contrast, a relational, democratic perspective seeks input and direction from members located throughout the organization. The leader-follower paradigm sees quality resulting from compliance with preestablished standards; the relational-democratic paradigm sees quality from empowerment and enterprise among diverse members of the organization. Thus graduate programs need to stress an understanding of the role of dialogue and group dynamics. Such an understanding may be advanced through formal courses focused on the social and cultural foundations of group behavior or by incorporating applicable case studies into already existing administration or organizational courses.

Create opportunities for underrepresented graduate students. As part of creating more inclusionary practices, graduate programs for community college leaders need to intentionally recruit and seek to retain members of underrepresented groups. If we desire to develop community college leaders who are committed to equal opportunity for all, then our graduate programs must embody those same values. Because mentoring is such an important factor in the success of students, special attention must be given to the mentoring process. Mentors (those who are not from underrepresented groups) need to be encouraged to step out of their "reproduction-of-self" comfort zones and welcome women and minorities as protegees.

Conclusion

Our position throughout this chapter is that leadership does not rest solely in the hands of the community college president and that faculty and staff have numerous opportunities throughout their organizational lives to serve as leaders. This expands the range of community college professionals that may benefit from graduate programs in community college education. Our vision of leadership moves away from the Great Man theory of past generations and emphasizes a more collaborative vision such as that offered by democratic notions of leadership and dialogic, relational visions of discourse. Programs preparing graduate students for positions in community colleges are challenged to develop future leaders who are capable of working with diverse constituents and are able to understand the complex and multiple meanings prevalent in today's community colleges. Without such an understanding, building cooperation and community is unlikely.

References

Amey, M. J., and Twombly, S. B. "Re-visioning Leadership in Community Colleges." *Review of Higher Education,* 1992, *15* (2), 125–150.

Baldridge, J. V. *Academic Governance: Research on Institutional Politics and Decision-Making.* Berkeley, Calif.: McCutchan, 1971.

Baxter, L., and Montgomery, B. *Relating: Dialectics and Dialogues.* New York: Guilford Press, 1996.

Bensimon, E. M. "The New President and Understanding the Campus as a Culture." In W. G. Tierney (ed.), *Assessing Academic Climates and Cultures.* New Directions for Institutional Research, no. 68. San Francisco: Jossey-Bass, 1990.

Bensimon, E. M. (ed.). *Multicultural Teaching and Learning.* University Park, Pa.: National Center on Postsecondary Teaching, Learning, & Assessment, 1994.

Bensimon, E. M., Neumann, A., and Birnbaum, R. *Making Sense of Administrative Leadership: The "L" Word in Higher Education.* ASHE-ERIC Higher Education Report, No. 1. Washington, D.C.: Association for the Study of Higher Education, 1989.

Bolman, L. G., and Deal, T. E. *Reframing Organizations: Artistry, Choice, and Leadership.* San Francisco: Jossey-Bass 1991.

Capozzoloi, M. J. *A Survey of Women Community College Administrators.* Princeton, N.J.: Princeton University, 1989. (ED 307 930)

Chaffee, E. E., and Tierney, W. G. *Collegiate Culture and Leadership Strategies.* New York: American Council on Education/Macmillan, 1988.

Clark, B. R. "The Organizational Saga in Higher Education." *Administrative Science Quarterly,* 1972, *17,* 179–194.

Clark, B. R. *The Academic Life: Small Worlds, Different Worlds.* Princeton, N.J.: Carnegie Foundation for the Advancement of Teaching, 1987.

Dewey, J. *Democracy and Education.* Carbondale: Southern Illinois University, 1916.

Fulton, B. F. "Access for Minorities and Women to Administrative Leadership Positions: Influence of the Search Committee." *Journal of the National Association for Women Deans, Administrators, and Counselors,* 1984, *48* (1), 3–7.

Gergen, K. "Relational Leadership." Presentation at the 1995 Taos Institute on Relational Leadership, Taos, N.M., Oct. 1995.

Gibson-Benninger, B. S., and Ratcliff, J. L. "Getting and Keeping the Best Faculty for the Twenty-First-Century Community College." *Community College Journal of Research and Practice,* 1996, *20,* 151–167.

Gillett-Karam, R., Roueche, S. D., and Roueche, J. E. *Underrepresentation and the Question of Diversity, Women, and Minorities in the Community College.* Washington D.C.: American Association of Community and Junior Colleges, 1991.

Gleazer, E. J. *This Is the Community College.* New York: Houghton Mifflin, 1968.

Goodman, P. *The Community of Scholars.* New York: Random House, 1962.

Goodwin, G. L. "The Historical Development of Community College Ideology: An Analysis and Interpretation of the Writings of Selected Community-College National Leaders from 1890–1970." Unpublished doctoral dissertation, University of Illinois, 1971.

Havelock, R., and others. *Planning for Innovation Through the Dissemination and Utilization of Scientific Knowledge.* Ann Arbor: Institute for Social Research, University of Michigan, 1971.

Kuh, G., and Whitt, E. J. *The Invisible Tapestry: Culture in American Colleges and Universities.* ASHE-ERIC Higher Education Report No. 1. Washington, D.C.: Association for the Study of Higher Education, 1988.

Lindquist, J. *Strategies for Change.* Berkeley, Calif.: Pacific Soundings Press, 1978.

Montgomery, B. "The Relationship Between Higher Education and Society: A Dialogic Perspective on the Autonomy/Connection Contradiction." Paper presented at the annual forum of the European Association for Institutional Research, Zurich, Switzerland, Aug. 1995.

Morgan, G. *Images of Organization.* Thousand Oaks, Calif.: Sage, 1986.

Parsons, M. H. "Quo Vadis: Staffing the People's College 2000." In K. Kroll (ed.), *Maintaining Faculty Excellence.* New Directions for Community Colleges, no. 79. San Francisco: Jossey-Bass, 1992.

Ratcliff, J. L. "First Public Junior Colleges in an Age of Reform." *Journal of Higher Education,* 1987a, *58* (2), 151–180.

Ratcliff, J. L. "Should We Forget William Rainey Harper?" *Community College Review,* 1987b, *13* (4), 12–19.

Rhoads, R. A., and Tierney, W. G. *Cultural Leadership in Higher Education.* University Park, Pa.: National Center for Postsecondary Teaching, Learning & Assessment, 1992.

Rhoads, R. A., and Valadez, J. R. *Democracy, Multiculturalism, and the Community College: A Critical Perspective.* New York: Garland, 1996.

Richardson, R. C., Blocker, C. E., and Bender, L. W. *Governance for the Two-Year College.* Englewood Cliffs, N.J.: Prentice Hall, 1972.

Rogers, E. M., and Rogers, R. A. *Communications in Organizations.* New York: Free Press, 1976.

Roueche, J. E., Baker, G. A., III, and Rose, R. R. *Shared Vision: Transformational Leadership in American Community Colleges.* Washington, D.C.: Community College Press, 1989.

Schneider, A. M. "Mentoring Women and Minorities into Positions of Educational Leadership: Gender Differences and Implications for Mentoring." Paper presented at the annual conference of the National Council of States on In-Service Education, Houston, Tex., Nov. 1991.

Shafer, R. J. (ed.). *A Guide to Historical Method.* Homewood, Ill.: Dorsey Press, 1974.

Tierney, W. G. "Organizational Culture in Higher Education." *Journal of Higher Education,* 1988, *59* (1), 2–21.

Tierney, W. G. *Building Communities of Difference: Higher Education in the Twenty-First Century.* New York: Bergin & Garvey, 1993.

Vaughan, G. B. *Leadership in Transition: The Community College Presidency.* New York: American Council on Education/Macmillan, 1989.

BARBARA S. GIBSON-BENNINGER *is a graduate research assistant at the Center for the Study of Higher Education at The Pennsylvania State University in University Park, Pennsylvania.*

JAMES L. RATCLIFF *is director of the Center for the Study of Higher Education and a professor at The Pennsylvania State University in University Park, Pennsylvania.*

ROBERT A. RHOADS *is an assistant professor in the Department of Educational Administration at Michigan State University in Lansing, Michigan.*

The professoriate of graduate programs that prepare community college leaders has employed the traditional roles of scholarship, teaching, and service to influence practitioners. This analysis links the halcyon past to the quality-oriented future, concluding that it is no time to rest on our laurels.

Professors as Leaders Within the Community College Movement

George A. Baker III

The American community college has evolved into a complex organization with several mission components that have emerged in response to public demands and social changes. The cold war launch of *Sputnik* led to a national commitment to mass education. The technical revolution of the 1960s, 1970s, and 1980s signaled the importance of education beyond high school that would prepare thousands of practical engineers and technicians in hundreds of scientific areas. In addition, two-year college responses to the demands of businesses, four-year colleges, and government agencies resulted in structural changes and an expanded curriculum.

The evidence is strong that university professors specializing in community college education have also exercised significant influence on the institution throughout its evolution. Many university scholars, notably Koos and Eells, were key leaders of the early junior college movement. Since the 1940s, university professors have influenced organizational performance through research, educated many community college chief executive officers, and extended their influence into the field through consulting and other service activities. Surely, no group in America has been more influential in charting the direction of the community college movement.

Drawing on the writer's own experience, this chapter will examine the dynamics of this influence, noting the ways professors interact with and help prepare community college leaders. The author will attempt to analyze both the current approach to graduate education and suggest ways in which graduate programs should be able to meet the needs of their students into the twenty-first century. Such an analysis is necessary if we are to answer two key questions: How well has this professoriate served community colleges? and Are the graduate education formats established during the post–World War II growth period appropriate for the education of current and future community college leaders?

Context

This writer entered the community college movement in 1970 while on leave from the U.S. Marine Corps. He had served two tours in Vietnam and would serve his remaining military years in educational roles, training instructors and teaching management theory to military officers and government officials. In addition, he has taught organizational behavior to students pursuing master's degrees in business administration and public administration. From 1976 through 1978 he served as an administrator in a community college and from 1978 to the present as professor of higher and community college education, first at the University of Texas and since 1992 at North Carolina State University.

During the author's past twenty years of service, much has happened to bring a powerful spotlight to America's institutions of higher education. The American higher education enterprise has come under a growing crescendo of criticism from those claiming that higher education is more interested in expanding its power than in fulfilling its traditional roles of research, teaching, and service; that recruitment of ill-prepared students is common in all types of higher education institutions; and that tuition and fees are excessive, rising by an average of 2 percent more than inflation throughout the twentieth century (Finn and Manno, 1996). The critics argue that salaries are comfortable, workloads are down, and the average professor (all ranks) produces one article, a third of a book review, and two professional presentations per year (Wolfe, 1996). In response, the reform of higher education is under way. Budgets are being cut, workloads are being scrutinized, and outcome measures are being developed.

Undoubtedly, those of us who teach at major research universities will continue to account for our time, publish or fade into obscurity, and serve our former students and other clients in the field, just as we have in the past. My best vision is that professors in higher education will be required to reinforce teaching and advising skills and, especially in graduate programs, to produce the next generation of college administrators. Those who are leaders will need to be better managers and influencers than those who entered leadership positions in the 1960s, not because the first generation of leaders was inadequate but because the environments in which these new leaders will operate will be different. Institutions are larger, society is more complex, expectations have been elevated, and the general message from those who fund these institutions is, "Do more with less."

Since 1978, the writer has been fully involved in fulfilling the role of a university professor. His research agenda has been related to the field of management science, and he has served community colleges, state systems, and business and industry with one primary purpose: to produce leaders for community colleges and higher educational public and private institutions of America. This chapter is essentially about the writer's experience, perceptions, and assumptions and does not purport to be an empirical analysis of higher and community college professional programs in America. Experience has been a valuable teacher, and this writer is qualified to address the questions raised by the editors of this volume by generalizing from his experience to the national university programs that include an option in community college leadership. First, however, two research studies will be explored in order to provide a context for the discussion of the university professor as leader in the field of higher education.

The Perkins Study. James R. Perkins, now president of Blue Ridge Community College (Virginia), defended a dissertation in 1980 in which he examined the outcomes of twelve community college leadership programs sponsored by the W. K. Kellogg Foundation. He sought to determine whether former recipients of W. K. Kellogg fellowship awards assumed leadership positions in the community college field and exerted influence on the development of the community college field within higher education. He studied all living Kellogg fellows in the twelve supported community college leadership programs during the period 1960–1974. He identified 471 fellows and employed a questionnaire to determine career development and professional activities. He received responses from 339 fellows, 74 percent of the population. Ninety-eight of the respondents had achieved a presidency by 1979. In general, this group felt that they had been prepared or conditioned to respond to the issues of the 1960s, which focused on growth and development of the community college philosophy. However, less than half felt that they had been adequately prepared to deal with stable or declining resources.

Respondents also reported that the most valuable doctoral activities included contact with other students and faculty, course work, and the internship experience. Undoubtedly, the identical activities would be listed today by current community college graduate students and recent graduates. Respondents felt that research work and some of the specialization courses were less beneficial (Perkins, 1980, p. 163). Perkins reported that several community college leadership programs were recognized by a panel of experts as outstanding in the preparation of community college administrators.

The Keim Study. According to Keim (1992), over thirty-one programs in the United States offer master's or doctoral-level professional training for current or prospective community college leaders. These programs range from self-standing programs that specifically emphasize community college education (such as the programs at the University of Texas and North Carolina State University) to programs that cover educational administration generally without course titles that contain the words community college.

According to Keim, the professors in these programs have taught hundreds of graduate students, most of whom are currently working in community colleges. They have chaired to completion many doctoral dissertations and served on huge numbers of dissertation committees. Typically, they write letters of recommendation for former students, and in some cases they have seen former students move through two or more positions to the presidency of community colleges or the chancellorship of community college districts.

In my experience, professors have evaluated their students from the perspectives of personality, competency, and motivation. They have listened carefully to the competencies sought by search committees and have been advocates for their students when they apply for leadership positions. They have written proposals, developed models, conducted research, and analyzed results. They have published hundreds of books and monographs and thousands of chapters, articles, and technical reports. They have planned, developed, and led consortia ranging in size from the National Institute for Staff and Organizational Development (which includes six hundred colleges) to the National Alliance of Community and Technical Colleges (which has less than fifty members). They have served on the board of the American Association of Community Colleges and as committee chairs in the American Educational Research Association. They have served on school boards, corporate boards, and state, regional, and local boards. They have been visible, involved, and dedicated to achieving respect for the people's colleges.

It is clear that the professors in these programs have not only influenced community college leaders and followers, but also education and training for industry, education, and public service. What will be needed in the future is more empirically designed research so that the influence patterns can be ascertained and promulgated.

The Professoriate

To estimate how well these professorial activities have served practitioners in the field one first needs to describe the three major functions of the professoriate: teaching (including classroom instruction, course development, and mentoring), scholarship, and service. Typically, professors are evaluated for promotion, tenure, and merit based on their roles in these major areas. Each has a significant impact on community college leadership.

Classroom instruction. The most powerful way that professors influence the behavior of future leaders is through formal teaching. Professors should be very aware of this influence and recognize the necessity of modeling behavior that will be expected of their students. When this influence process is effective, students carry into the field the lessons learned in the graduate program. It is extremely difficult to influence future leaders by teaching one set of values and practicing another. In general, graduate students will lead the way they were led. Obviously of less value is to learn from their professors how not to lead.

Course development. Professors are expected to design courses that link theory to leadership practice. The most effective courses are those that are designed from a list of behaviors actually employed on the job. As course developer, the professor should design the course in ways that actively engage students in the learning process. Assigned readings can be employed for basic knowledge acquisition and classroom time can be used for the application of concepts, thereby allowing students to practice decision making and problem solving in as realistic a setting as possible. Since community college leaders are expected to lead their teams into collaborative problem solving, course strategies should follow a collaborative and team building classroom format (Baker, 1995, Chap. 11).

Leaders are expected to be thinkers, and the best way to develop thinking is to require the student to apply theory and solve problems through writing. Short written papers should be held to the same standard that would be expected in advanced written examinations and, ultimately, in dissertations. Students should be given many opportunities to express their thoughts in writing, and they should receive timely and detailed feedback on the quality of their written expression and organization. In a similar fashion, students should play many leadership roles with a variety of cases before being expected to perform on departmental written and oral examinations. A series of high expectations followed by rapid and accurate feedback will generally enhance student capacity to employ critical thinking in realistic leadership settings (Barnes, Christensen, and Hansen, 1994).

Advising and mentoring. Effective advising and mentoring are critical teaching roles expected of all full-time faculty members in a leadership program. In this writer's experience, it is here that theory and practice are explained, critiqued, analyzed, and evaluated and the greatest opportunity for influence exists. One-on-one teaching that helps students create a path to a critical goal has been found to transcend classroom instruction and result in high levels of performance and satisfaction on the part of the graduate student and the mentor.

It follows, therefore, that the assignment of advisors and mentors to graduate students should be the result of a carefully applied program. Advisors can be assigned on a temporary basis upon admission to the program. When the graduate student has completed a portion of the required course work, the early assignment of a permanent advisor or dissertation chair should result in a verbal, and eventually a written, contract between the dissertation advisor and the graduate student.

Scholarship. As a general rule, scholarship is defined as both the product or result of being educated and the quality or state of being erudite. It is obvious then that the professor should be a true expert in some aspect of the field of study in which he or she is a lifelong learner. In a leadership program, scholars should help graduate students become effective developers of high performance in individuals, units, and teams. One professor may specialize in organizational theory, another in student services, another in curriculum and instruction, and so on; yet all professors should be scholars in the erudite aspects of their specialization arenas.

Looking again at the Perkins study (1980), Kellogg fellows listed some of their own as individuals who had influenced their thinking. Richard Richardson, Dale Tillery, John Roueche, and Ervin Harlacher were noted by their peers as significant authors. (Arthur Cohen and Terry O'Banion were listed but not considered by Perkins as Kellogg fellows for the purpose of his study.) In 1990, Baker invited members of the Council of Universities and Colleges (CUC) to contribute chapters to the *Handbook on the Community College in America* (Baker, 1994). CUC professors who were cited in this volume more than ten times by other authors were Richard Alfred, George Baker, Florence Brawer, Arthur Cohen, K. Patricia Cross, William Deegan, Edmund Gleazer, S. V. Martorana, Leland Medsker, James Palmer, John Roueche, Dale Tillery, and George Vaughan. I believe these to be the writers who would emerge from a Perkins-type analysis of the 1970s and 1980s. Several new professors also developed chapters in *A Handbook on the Community College in America,* and many of these writers would appear on a list of influential writers of the 1990s. A few relatively new writers to the field of community college leadership are Rosemary Gillett-Karam, Robert Pedersen, Al Smith, Elizabeth Hawthorne, Laura Rendón, Suanne Roueche, Barbara Townsend, and James Valadez. It is uplifting to see both women and ethnic minorities contributing so powerfully and fully to the process of influencing the community college movement.

It is my belief that professors do influence practitioners through their research and scholarly efforts. One example is the book *Access and Excellence: The Open Door College* by Roueche and Baker (1987). This book was based on a case study of the top-ranked community college in America. The ranking was the result of the perceptions and opinions of fourteen CUC professors who were active at the time. Based on a five-point scale, Miami-Dade Community College amassed sixty-five points—and the second-ranked institution received eighteen points. Baker and Roueche, along with a research team, evaluated Miami-Dade's culture, management systems, leadership, and teaching effectiveness. Besides providing a foundation for further change at Miami-Dade, the book became a Community College Press best-seller for almost a decade. Community college presidents and their teams purchased the book and used it to implement many of the reforms undertaken at Miami-Dade. The volume undoubtedly was a major factor in ongoing efforts to link access and effectiveness in the American community college. But again, little research has been conducted to determine what effect publications from the Community College Press, Jossey-Bass, or other sources have on the behavior of leaders or managers who attempt to implement change by replicating what others report.

Several other books offer examples of professorial influence on practice. *The American Community College* by Cohen and Brawer (1982, 1989) was referenced more than any other single publication in *A Handbook on the Community College in America;* it was cited by almost one-third of the total chapter authors. Cohen and Brawer and a group of colleagues recently published *Managing Community Colleges* (1994). It is believed that this work will also heavily influence change because the orientation of the book is toward improved effectiveness in all functions of a community college. These and other books testify to the effort of university professors to describe and influence the community college enterprise, but only empirical research can determine the effect of these publications on practitioners and their organizations.

The service arena. Community colleges depend on consultants to bring outside and timely concepts to their campuses. Typically, professors are encouraged to invest one day per week in providing service to the field. Professors deliver service in a variety of ways. They provide motivational messages at major conferences and on various campuses. They conduct workshops to enhance the skills of individuals, units, and teams. They evaluate federal and state programs, recommending improvement where needed. Perhaps the greatest influence occurs when professors present research involving a college that has benefitted from their service and intervention. Most management theory has been developed for use in the profit sector, but professors typically translate these concepts into paradigms that fit the culture of the community college.

Several professors of adult, higher, and community college education have led consortia designed to improve community college services. Project ACCLAIM at North Carolina State University (NCSU), the League for Innovation, the National Alliance of Community and Technical Colleges (at NCSU), the National Initiative for Leadership and Institutional Effectiveness (University of Texas, Austin), the National Institute for Staff and Organizational Development (University of Texas, Austin), and the Community College Consortium (University of Michigan) are examples (to name a few). They provide tremendous assistance to the twelve hundred or so community colleges in America.

One example of the service role worthy of note is the research component of the National Initiative for Leadership and Institutional Effectiveness (NILIE), which is operated by the Department of Adult and Community College Education at NCSU. Member community colleges can use NILIE's home page on the World Wide Web to report action science change strategies that might be used as models for other institutions. NILIE also conducts a series of climate studies that analyze work group perceptions of various college operations and help educational institutions develop strategies for improving effectiveness. Graduate students under the direction of an NCSU professor develop the research studies and manage the World Wide Web home page.

Numerous other examples could be cited. James Ratcliff of the Center for the Study of Higher Education at Pennsylvania State University edits a reader on community colleges for the Association for the Study of Higher Education. John and Suanne Roueche at the University of Texas, Austin, along with a group of graduate students and colleagues, have published on average a book a year since the 1980s. The National Institute for Staff and Organizational Development, which they have led, serves more than six hundred colleges worldwide. Arthur Cohen of the University of California, Los Angeles, has operated the ERIC Clearinghouse for Community Colleges for three decades. No serious professor or graduate student would begin a major research study or develop an article without conducting a search of the ERIC database. Surely all these efforts have had an impact on the production of new research, but without further study, the direction and strength of this impact is not known.

Situational Ethics: Placing a Priority on Students

Research, teaching, and service, the three-legged foundation of the university professor, are obviously linked. The more one engages in research, the more likely one is to receive research funding. On the other hand, the more one conducts research, the less one is available to students. The more one publishes, the more one is in demand for consulting opportunities. The more time one spends in the field, the less likely one is to be available when students need help. The obvious solution to this challenge is to make teaching and advising the first priority.

Professors can do this without sacrificing involvement in scholarship and field service by including graduate students in their research agendas. Generally, those students who conduct research with their professors share in the rewards for such efforts and often have the opportunity to present research findings in the classroom or at professional conferences. Although professors are expected to show strength in all these areas, the major purpose of a professor of higher or community college education is the development of the next generation of community college leaders.

Community college presidents have never had a tougher time than they do today. Yet these leaders were trained in our leadership programs and have performed extremely well in the toughest of times. They as a group have found the courage to articulate the mission, to keep the doors open, and to influence the legislators who pay the bills. The next generation of community college leaders will find it even tougher to survive in a climate of cutbacks and retrenchment. They, more than the previous generations, will need the support of their graduate professors; they will need new research and the knowledge that their leadership teams are adequately prepared to meet the growing challenges that face institutions providing adult and continuing education. In my experience, the publication of books and articles helps to shape strategies for change. In addition, professors can provide advice and consulting, where needed.

Professors must be looked upon as ethical paragons by their students, and as sources of moral strength and courage. The professors thus must study various concepts and theories and be aware of the effect of their moral actions on their students. Professors of community college leadership have played and will continue to play major roles in the shaping of the community college movement. We should all be guided by Burns's words: "The ultimate test of moral leadership is its capacity to transcend . . . everyday wants and needs and expectations of followers, to respond to higher levels of moral development, and to relate leadership behavior . . . to a set of reasoned, relatively explicit, conscious values" (1978, p. 46).

Conclusion

This author was asked to answer the questions, "How do professors of community college leadership influence practitioners in the field, and how well do the university programs meet the needs of the next generation of community college leaders?" The ad hoc evidence is strong that professors of community college or higher education leadership have played a major role in the history of the community college movement, although little empirical research exists to support this conclusion. These professors operate often as the single community college expert in a department of educational administrators, adult educators, or other social scientists. In larger programs, they function as a team, but hardly ever hold enough votes to carry a major issue in their departments.

To continue to serve, professors must reinvent themselves every year. They must find a way to regularly bring new and refreshing research to their students and the practitioners. They must carry out research in the field and return to the field to present research to a grateful audience. They must continue to graduate hundreds of community college leaders who often immediately join the ranks of the senior leadership team in a community college. They must establish lifelong relationships with their former students. They must continue to bring with them new decision models, new problem-solving techniques, and new ways of influencing the behavior of followers. In a forward-looking program, they must continue to model effective leadership and develop systematic and motivational instruction. They must continue to prove that they can use the scientific method to identify and bring new knowledge to the challenge of solving new and continuing problems.

It is a rare situation when graduate students have not established a lifelong relationship with their major professor and mentor. Professors who would desire to influence their students for life must keep their students as their first priority. The quality of early relationships sets the tone for everything to follow. A friendly but firm directive leadership strategy anchored in moral development theory gives way to a coaching relationship as the graduate student matures. The opportunity to write together in a true partnership is perhaps the greatest evidence of mutual respect and ultimate benefit to both parties.

But the constant demonstration of respect for individual differences is crucial for a lifetime of mutual admiration and support. The wise professor, when asked how she accumulated so much wisdom, answered "one graduate student at a time!" Professors of higher education, community college leadership, adult education, and educational administration have been, since the beginning of the community college movement, the major forces in moving this new, innovative model forward. Undoubtedly, they will continue to do so in the future. I would not classify these professors as heroes in the classical sense, but surely no other group has had so much influence in the literature in shaping a uniquely American phenomenon.

References

Baker, G. A., III. *Handbook on the Community College in America*. Westport, Conn.: Greenwood Press, 1994.

Baker, G. A., III. *Team Building for Quality: Transitions in the American Community College.* Washington, D.C.: Community College Press, 1995.

Barnes, L., Christensen, C., and Hansen, A. *Teaching and the Case Method.* Boston: Harvard Business School Press, 1994.

Burns, J. *Leadership.* New York: HarperCollins, 1978.

Cohen, A., and Brawer, F. *The American Community College.* San Francisco: Jossey-Bass, 1982.

Cohen, A., and Brawer, F. *The American Community College.* (2nd ed.) San Francisco: Jossey-Bass, 1989.

Cohen, A., Brawer, F., and Associates. *Managing Community Colleges in America: A Handbook for Effective Practice.* San Francisco: Jossey-Bass, 1994.

Finn, C., and Manno, B. "What's Wrong With the American University?" *Wilson Quarterly,* 1996, *20* (1), 44–53.

Gleazer, E. J., Jr. "The Evolution of Junior Colleges into Community Colleges." In G. A. Baker III (ed.), *A Handbook on the Community College in America.* Westport, Conn.: Greenwood Press, 1994.

Keim, M. C. *Directory of Graduate Preparation Programs in Community College Education, Council of Universities and Colleges.* Washington, D.C.: American Association of Community Colleges, 1992.

Perkins, J. R. "An Outcomes Analysis of the Preservice Fellowship Recipients of the W.K. Kellogg Foundation Supported Junior College Leadership Program." Unpublished doctoral dissertation, Department of Educational Leadership, Florida State University, 1980.

Roueche, J., and Baker, G. A., III. *Access and Excellence.* Washington, D.C.: Community College Press, 1987.

Wolfe, A. "The Feudal Culture of the Postmodern University." *Wilson Quarterly,* 1996, 20 (1), 54–66.

GEORGE A. BAKER III *is the Joseph D. Moore Distinguished Professor of Community College Leadership and director of the National Initiative for Leadership and Institutional Effectiveness in the Department of Adult and Community College Education, College of Education and Psychology, North Carolina State University, Raleigh, North Carolina.*

Professors of community college education work with and study a particular institution, but they are not of the institution per se. They serve community college educators best by avoiding advocacy, understanding the limited vocational utility of university studies, and providing intellectual frameworks that prevent the institution from becoming an end unto itself.

The Transactional Relationship Between University Professors and Community College Leaders

James C. Palmer

University professors specializing in community colleges trace the roots of their profession to the emergence of higher education as a specialized field of graduate study. The early development of graduate classes in higher education administration at such institutions as the Ohio State University and the University of Chicago coincided with the emergence of junior colleges in the first decades of the century, and courses preparing leaders for these new institutions were among the first to be offered (Goodchild, 1991). The post–World War II expansion of community colleges intensified the need for administrators and spurred the development of specialized doctoral programs, notably the Junior College Leadership programs that were subsidized by the Kellogg Foundation (Dressel and Mayhew, 1974; Morgan and Newell, 1982).

Today the demand for new college administrators is less urgent, but a small professoriate devoted to the study of community colleges remains. Approximately fifty university professors currently belong to the Council of Universities and Colleges, which is affiliated with the American Association of Community Colleges. These professors, almost all of whom hold positions in colleges or graduate schools of education, devote themselves to analyses of the community college for its own sake and are to be distinguished from scholars in other disciplines (such as sociology) who use the community college as a lens through which theoretical perspectives in the social sciences may be studied. The work of these community college specialists has been documented in a small body of literature that catalogues the number and types of universities that offer graduate courses on community college education or administration

(Lumsden and Stewart, 1992), describes the graduate programs designed specifically for community college leaders (Keim, 1994), comments on the quality of those programs (Richardson, 1987), and surveys the attitudes, values, and practices of program faculty and graduates (Morgan and Newell, 1982; Townsend and Wiese, 1990; Hawthorne and Ninke, 1991).

The institutional focus of the community college specialist, however, poses a difficult challenge that is rarely addressed in the literature: how to combine the role of objective analyst or observer of the community college with the role of participant in the community college enterprise. Indeed, the professor's relationship with the subject of inquiry—people in community colleges—is as transactional as it is analytic. University scholars in this arena depend on the cooperation of community college educators for data and hope that these same professionals will find their research and teaching helpful in strengthening the community college's educational impact. Besides attending to the tenets of scholarship (such as probity in data collection, interpretation, and reporting), the university professor entering into this transactional relationship requires a clear sense of what he or she can and is willing to offer community college educators.

This chapter offers and defends a set of premises about the nature and limits of professorial obligations to practitioners. It reflects the attempt of a relatively new professor to define his scholarly work and is based on the overarching assumption that the professor specializing in community college education is not simply a student of the community college per se, but a student of education within the institutional setting of the community college. From this perspective, professorial work entails three imperatives: it is analytic and should not serve the cause of institutional advocacy, seeking only to increase the resources available to the community college or to defend the institution against its critics; it engages students on an intellectual rather than vocational basis; and it contributes to a well-defined graduate curriculum that is constructed around one or more scholarly themes, such as educational leadership, social science inquiry, or curriculum theory. All are crucial to the stability of an academic field that must, as Richardson (1987) notes, balance "the values and priorities of community college leaders. . . [with] university values in research and scholarship" (p. 41).

Avoiding Advocacy

University professors of community college education walk a fine line between scholarship and institutional advocacy. The former rests on objective criticism while the latter entails partisan promotion aimed at defending the community college as an institution and increasing the resources available to it. Given the close ties between professors and the community colleges they study, the two may be easily confounded. Indeed, many of the first scholars in this discipline, notably Koos and Eells, were associated with the development of the junior college, and many contemporary professors began their professional careers as community college practitioners.

The boundary between scholarship and advocacy is not always clear. But the professor will know he or she has encountered it when relations with practitioners threaten to go awry. An example, drawn from the writer's own experience, lies in the conflicting interests that can emerge when a community college contracts with a professor to conduct a program evaluation or other type of study on its behalf. The professor's desire to publish the findings may be met with the college's insistence on the right of prior approval to any publication. Although acquiescence to this demand may reflect an honest desire to help the college by placing its needs ahead of the academy's, it makes the professor a partner in institutional advocacy. Perversely, research becomes private as the fear of adverse publicity (should the evaluation reveal flaws) overrides the pursuit of knowledge. Without uniform exposure to what Argyris (1993, p. 74) aptly calls "the marketplace of academic and practitioner scrutiny," research quality suffers and the professor's capacity to help college practitioners declines.

The boundary between scholarship and advocacy may also be recognized when the professor, mindful of the community college's long history of institutional defensiveness, hesitates to criticize the community college in the classroom or in his or her writings. The writer has experienced this defensiveness in his own courses when students (usually community college educators) are required to read articles and books that are critical of the institution. The initial anger of the students must be dispelled with the disclaimer that criticisms are not attacks on the institution and that criticisms leveled at community colleges might just as easily be leveled at the university. This is an endemic, decades-old problem. Cohen (1969) recognized the necessity of dealing with anger and defensiveness in the introduction to *Dateline '79: Heretical Concepts for the Community College*. "In the course of my work," he noted, "I speak with junior college faculty members and administrators in most areas of the United States. On occasion, I find fault with their practices and, when I do, I am invariably met with the accusation, 'You are another!' Not until they are satisfied that I recognize the shortcomings in my own teaching and the inadequacies of the university with which they are affiliated will they attend to my arguments" (p. vii).

It would be a gross oversimplification to characterize professors as uniformly objective observers pitted against overly zealous institutional partisans. Some of the institutional defensiveness exhibited by practitioners may indeed be a reaction to shoddy university research; Vaughan (1980) correctly notes that the detachment of university professors from the community college enterprise does not guarantee objectivity. But this does not obviate the danger that professors, fearful of alienation from the very people they depend on as a source of students and research data, will not examine or describe the community college in an objective manner. To the extent that this happens, the community college forgoes the insights that can potentially be brought to bear by outside observers. It also shields the status quo from scrutiny and hence places the professor unwittingly in the role of advocate, helping to perpetuate rather than improve current educational practices.

Stressing Intellectual as Opposed to Vocational Ends

A related problem lies in the tendency of some practitioners to urge a vocationally oriented graduate curriculum, stressing administrative competencies rather than intellectual inquiry. This vocationalism emerges when community college practitioners argue for *relevant* graduate programming and define relevance in terms of day-to-day college operations. For example, community college administrators responding to a survey conducted by Townsend and Wiese (1990) rated courses in budget, finance, organization, and governance as essential to the preparation of graduates. Courses on college teaching or on the history and philosophy of the community college were not considered essential, presumably because they had little bearing on the day-to-day tasks faced by the respondents.

Given the administrative pressures faced by practitioners, the emphasis on vocationalism is understandable. In addition, vocationalism is deeply rooted in the history of graduate programs in higher education, which gained a secure place in the university structure only when informal routes to leadership positions (by which teachers or school administrators gradually advanced through the ranks) broke down in the face of skyrocketing demand for administrators in the 1950s and 1960s (Dressel and Mayhew, 1974). Job-getting reigned supreme: "The most successful programs of the sixties were those that got people on the job quickly" (Richardson, 1987, p. 40).

But the vocational emphasis can be self-defeating. It stresses and hence may perpetuate the status quo, doing little to encourage an ethos of critical analysis. Its bureaucratic orientation may inadequately prepare community college leaders to define and communicate the educational purpose of their institutions, intellectual tasks that Vaughan (1989) notes are the college president's first obligation. In addition, an emphasis on vocationalism implicitly oversells the university's educative capacity, which rests more on the development of general intellectual skills applicable to a wide range of situations than on the mastery of job tasks. Given the ever-changing and idiosyncratic contexts of specific administrative positions, university promises to ease students into administrative slots may become disingenuous.

This does not mean that universities should remain aloof. Class discussions and assignments can (and should) help students draw links between theory and practice. In addition, internships can play an important role in helping students apply knowledge gained to specific settings (Townsend and Wiese, 1990). But the broader aims of graduate education should be articulated and defended. Speaking at New York University's 1993 Symposium on the Urban Community College, Arthur Cohen offered a five-part agenda, arguing that the graduate programs that will serve prospective community college leaders best will be those that:

1. Help students recognize and take informed stands on the intractable problems and perennial issues in education;

2. provide a model of scholastic and professional integrity;
3. connect students with a network of practitioners through internships and participation in conferences;
4. insist on widespread reading in history, biography, anthropology, and other disciplines that frame the institutional context of the community college; and
5. have a focus within [themselves], such as research, multi-cultural education, or any other special emphasis [quoted in Palmer, 1993, p. 7].

While the curriculum developed according to these or similar principles will not prepare the student for a specific job, it embodies aims that the university is designed to achieve and it has the potential to help students place their day-to-day work in a broader context.

Defining the Intellectual Focus

Cohen's fifth principle—the need for a unifying focus in the curriculum—has eluded the academic field of higher education. While graduate programs in higher education properly borrow from a variety of disciplines, the nature of higher education as "a distinct field of study" remains uncertain, as do the boundaries of that field (whatever it may be) with other disciplines (Dressel and Mayhew, 1974, p. 7; Fulton, 1992, p. 1810). This can only add to the confusion about the obligations of professors to community college colleagues, especially in the absence of an urgent need to fill administrative slots at new institutions (a need that drove graduate programs through the 1960s).

It is unlikely that all graduate programs preparing community college educators will adopt the same intellectual focus. Nor is such unity necessary. But it is important for faculty within individual programs to specify the intellectual foundations on which they work, be it leadership theory, curriculum theory, research methodology, or some other framework that helps define what Hutchins (1967 [1936], p. 46) called the "intellectual problems of the profession," those that are not unique to particular institutional settings and that place the community college in a broader perspective. For example, serious study of administrative theory can help college leaders trace the influence of Frederick Taylor on the design and management of schools and colleges in the twentieth century, thereby providing a sense of how managerial theories from the business world are adapted and used (or misused) by educators. This may help college leaders assess the usefulness of the many approaches to administration and leadership that are often superficially described in the literature and at professional conferences.

Attention to curriculum theory can be equally helpful, because the community college is yet one more example of the age-old and continuing effort to create organizations that cause learning. Indeed, the intellectual roots of the community college as an educational enterprise did not emerge independently with the institution. Rather, they continue a long line of inquiry into the ends and means of education generally. In this century, that inquiry can be traced in the rise and fall of John Dewey's progressivism, in the development and use of Ralph Tyler's outcomes-based approach to curriculum development, in the counterarguments of Elliot Eisner and other scholars who advocate a less-directed approach to curriculum planning, and in other attempts to conceptualize and implement programs of study for students within institutional settings. (See Kliebard, 1992, for essays on the history of curriculum inquiry in the United States.) The community college leader who remains unaware of this heritage cannot orchestrate or explain the institution's educational work and may be unduly subject to recurrent educational fads. His or her expressions of devotion to teaching as an ideal will do little to promote the institution in the eyes of a public that is increasingly skeptical of the capacity of colleges to produce desired educational results.

Numerous intellectual frameworks besides administrative and curriculum theory could be used. But regardless of the scholarly focus, it must be defined and defended as educationally sound. For unlike the biologist, the historian, or the mathematician, the professor who claims a focus on an institution (in this case the community college) says little about his or her research and teaching and hence little about what he or she offers students and the practitioner community. Now that the era of growth for community colleges is over, the continued viability of the small professoriate specializing in community colleges will depend on how well it articulates and acts on a meaningful scholarly agenda.

Implications for Professorial Work

Professors of community college education work with and study a particular institution, but they are not themselves part of that institution. They serve community college educators best by avoiding advocacy, understanding the limited vocational utility of university studies, and providing intellectual frameworks that prevent the institution from becoming an end unto itself. Professorial transactions with community college colleagues should help them step outside of the day-to-day workings of the institution and view it from a detached and reflective perspective. This is particularly important as most public community colleges enter their fourth decade of operation and become increasingly a part of the educational status quo.

Accordingly, professors and practitioners need to determine their respective spheres of action, deciding where those spheres properly intersect and where they do not. Consulting arrangements with individual colleges (often conducted under the rubric of university service to the profession) are a case in point. Professors can insist on the right of unfettered publication while at the same time remaining sensitive to individuals within the college. Argyris (1993) offers a useful approach. When he conducts research for an organization, he insists on the right to publish the findings. Members of the organization have an opportunity to suggest revisions before publication, but they are not granted the freedom to veto the publication. If disagreements persist after the manuscript has been reviewed, the organization is granted space within the publication to include its views. "As a scholar and a member of a university faculty," Argyris notes, "I had an obligation to the stock of basic knowledge, but in doing so, I did not want to harm the organization" (p. 74).

The need to define respective roles applies to teaching as well. Sensitivity to practitioner demands for applied studies need not lead to the vocationalization of graduate curricula. Instead, the details of how to perform specific administrative jobs might best be left to occasional internships, on-the-job training, or continuing education offerings administered separately from degree programs. Interactions with practitioners should clarify the boundaries between university-based doctoral education and the learning opportunities that are best carried out in other arenas and formats. Signal examples of other learning formats are described by Laden in Chapter Five. The university can strengthen its intellectual foundation (and its capacity to educate community college leaders) by recognizing its limits and respecting the contributions that practitioners themselves can make toward their continuing education.

In the end, each professor needs to determine for him or herself where the boundaries of professorial obligations to practitioners lie. But with that determination comes the obligation to do sound scholarly work. Meaningful transactions with practitioners will not emerge if professorial comments on or criticisms of the community college are based on faulty assumptions and blithely offered as grand truth. The misuse of the so-called *cooling-out theory,* which Clark (1980) notes has been perversely interpreted by some as a uniform and proven characteristic of all community colleges rather than as a hypothesis that might be applicable to some institutions under certain circumstances, is a classic example. Such gross generalizations naturally lead to skepticism, if not justified anger, among community college practitioners. A healthy relationship with these practitioners will require professors to approach their work with an appropriate humility, recognizing the extreme limitations of social science research despite its methodological trimmings.

References

Argyris, C. *Knowledge for Action: A Guide to Overcoming Barriers to Organizational Change.* San Francisco: Jossey-Bass, 1993.

Clark, B. R. "The 'Cooling-Out' Function Revisited." In G. B. Vaughan (ed.), *Questioning the Community College Role.* New Directions for Community Colleges, no. 32. San Francisco: Jossey-Bass, 1980.

Cohen, A. M. *Dateline '79: Heretical Concepts for the Community College.* Beverly Hills: Glencoe Press, 1969.

Dressel, P. L., and Mayhew, L. B. *Higher Education as a Field of Study.* San Francisco: Jossey-Bass, 1974.

Fulton, O. "Higher Education Studies." In B. R. Clark and G. R. Neave (eds.), *The Encyclopedia of Higher Education,* Vol. 3. New York: Pergamon Press, 1992.

Goodchild, L. F. "Higher Education as a Field of Study: Its Origins, Programs, and Purposes, 1893–1960." In J. D. Fife and L. F. Goodchild (eds.), *Administration as a Profession.* New Directions for Higher Education, no. 76. San Francisco: Jossey-Bass, 1991.

Hawthorne, E. M., and Ninke, D. "A Focus on University Faculty Service to Community Colleges." *Community College Review,* 1991, *19* (1), 30–35.

Hutchins, R. M. *The Higher Learning in America.* (13th printing) New Haven, Conn.: Yale University Press, 1967. (Originally published 1936.)

Keim, M. C. "Graduate Preparation Programs in Community College Education." *Community College Review,* 1994, *22* (1), 53–61.

Kliebard, H. M. (ed.). *Forging the American Curriculum: Essays in Curriculum History and Theory.* New York: Routledge, 1992.

Lumsden, D. B., and Stewart, G. B. "American Colleges and Universities Offering Course Work on Two-Year Institutions: Results of a National Survey." *Community College Review,* 1992, *19* (4), 34–46.

Morgan, D. A., and Newell, L. J. "Professors of Community College Education: Changes in Theoretical and Professional Orientations." *Community/Junior College Quarterly of Research and Practice,* 1982, 7 (1), 15–29.

Palmer, J. "New York University Symposium on Urban Community Colleges (New York, New York, April 1–2, 1993)." Unpublished paper, 1993. (ED 357 775)

Richardson, R. C., Jr. "A Question of Quality: University Programs for Community College Leaders." *Community, Technical, and Junior College Journal,* 1987, 57 (4), 39–41.

Townsend, B. K., and Wiese, M. "Value of the Higher Education Doctorate For Community College Administrators." *Community/Junior College Quarterly of Research and Practice,* 1990, *14* (4), 337–347.

Vaughan, G. B. "Critics of the Community College: An Overview." In G. B. Vaughan (ed.), *Questioning the Community College Role.* New Directions for Community Colleges, no. 32. San Francisco: Jossey-Bass, 1980.

Vaughan, G. B. *Leadership in Transition: The Community College Presidency.* New York: American Council on Education/Macmillan, 1989.

JAMES C. PALMER *is associate professor of educational administration and foundations at Illinois State University, Normal.*

This chapter relates the points raised in this volume to previous
literature, focusing on the aims of graduate preparation programs
for community college leaders and the difficulties that sometimes
emerge in professor-practitioner relations.

Sources and Information: Graduate and Continuing Education for Community College Leaders

James C. Palmer, Stephen G. Katsinas

The preceding chapters add to a small body of literature on graduate and continuing education for community college leaders. Much of this literature is descriptive. ERIC documents and journal articles have occasionally catalogued the syllabi of selected graduate courses on community college education or proffered national listings of these courses and the universities that offer them (Alfred, 1986; Lumsden, 1981; Lumsden and Stewart, 1992a, 1992b; Miller and Nelson, 1993; Ratcliff, 1986). Descriptions of university programs for community college educators have also appeared (Academy for Community College Leadership, Advancement, Innovation, and Modeling, 1992; Rahaim, 1983; Wallenfeldt and Anglin, 1990; Vaughan, 1989).

Some authors, however, have ventured into critical or normative analysis. Their works investigate the strengths and weaknesses of professional education for community college leaders and reflect on what that education should entail. The picture that emerges is one of a graduate field with indistinct parameters. For example, Keim (1994) analyzed fifty-eight graduate preparation programs in community college education, suggesting (among other findings) that wide variations in admissions and degree requirements—as well as in the ways programs are described by universities—reflect a need for the development of standards that will bring consistency to the field.

Further investigation of the literature, including the chapters in this volume, suggests that uncertainties in our field pivot on at least two interrelated issues. One is program intent. Debates here focus on the desired ends of the education offered by graduate programs that prepare community college leaders. The second issue lies in the ongoing controversy about the nature of professor-practitioner relations, particularly when practitioner expectations for professorial action diverge from the expectations of the academy. Both issues have long dogged the field of higher education as an academic specialty (Dressel and Mayhew, 1974; Goodchild, 1991).

Program Intent

Discussions of program intent offer varying notions of the aims of graduate preparation programs for community college leaders. Authors have described program ends in terms of administrative competencies, desired personality traits, and the social goals of racial and gender equity. Richardson (1987, p. 41) notes that the result is confusion over the value of the graduate credential: "There is no shortage in the number of individuals who hold doctorates in community college leadership. What is missing is any common agreement about the competencies such a degree should imply. As one consequence, the degree is a limited asset both to the holder and the potential employer. One looks first at personal characteristics, second at the institution where the degree was earned, and then only incidently at the degree itself."

Part of the confusion about program ends can be traced to the nature of administrative work at community colleges. As Chapter Four demonstrates, college leaders require a wide-ranging repertoire of managerial and analytic skills. For example, Fryer (1984) suggests that successful administrators should be schooled in the history of the community college, in the nature of human behavior within organizations, and in the dynamics of group work. His outline of needed competencies also includes knowledge of research methods, planning, financial management, law, and personnel administration. In addition, he places great emphasis on the leader's capacity to assess and change his or her own values and beliefs, a quality emphasized in Chapter Three, where Vaughan and Scott note the link between writing skills and critical thinking ability. Other competencies stressed by contributors to this volume include the ability to understand organizational cultures (Chapter Seven), apply curriculum theory (Chapter Nine), and describe institutional differences between community colleges in meaningful ways (Chapter Two).

Taught competencies, however, are not the only program ends espoused by commentators. Some focus on the psychological traits of successful leaders and the social goals of increased opportunity for the participation of women and minorities in educational leadership. The former is evident in Chapter Eight, which notes that professors have an obligation to model the ethical behavior expected of educational leaders. Chapter Eight goes beyond the question of what the alumni of graduate programs should know, speculating on the type of people they should become and on the ways professors might enhance students' personal development.

Social ends come to the fore in this volume in Chapters Six and Seven. Noting the importance of the doctorate as a required credential for educational leaders, Chapter Six argues that professors are gatekeepers for the profession, determining who is admitted to and graduated from doctoral programs. The author stresses professors' obligation to assure the inclusion of women and minorities and to teach in ways that help students learn the effects of cultural and gender differences on the dynamics of administrative teams. Chapter Seven also stresses the inclusion of people from diverse backgrounds in educational settings, maintaining that graduate programs should help college leaders understand and apply principles of democratic administration that value wide-ranging participation in decision making. Both chapters stress professorial obligations to further gender and racial equity, suggesting that the outcomes of graduate education lie in a changed higher education enterprise generally and not just in the competencies of individual students.

But all discussions of desired program ends beg the question of actual professorial influence. How and to what degree do graduate preparation programs influence the character of their graduates, shape the nature of community college governance, or change institutional cultures in ways that stress contemporary concerns for multiculturalism? The answer is unclear, especially when one considers that the graduate education experienced by administrators is only one of the influences that shape the nature of the community college enterprise. As Chapter One points out, graduate preparation programs established in the post–World War II era were not subject to rigorous evaluation. Occasional studies have examined educator perceptions of the value of graduate degrees from such programs. For example, Townsend and Wiese (1990) surveyed a national sample of community college administrators, finding a wide range of opinions about the value of a doctorate in higher education as preparation for administrative work. But more detailed investigations of how graduate preparation programs have influenced community college leaders and their institutions have yet to be conducted.

Professor-Practitioner Relations

The nature of relations between university professors and the community college administrators they work with may also affect professorial influence. While Chapter Eight posits a close relationship between practitioners and professors, arguing that the latter have often served as role models and leaders in the community college movement, Chapter Nine notes the potentially conflicting interests of the two groups, suggesting that the professor's role as university scholar must not be compromised by the temptation to take on the role of institutional advocate, despite pressures to do so from the practitioners who are the subject of the professor's research. Graduate preparation programs can thus be viewed as part of a complex and sometimes troubled exchange between community college and university educators.

The diverse and urgent day-to-day problems faced by college administrators play a role in this exchange. Practitioners seek assistance from the university in coping with on-the-job issues, but they may be disappointed by the response. Examining surveys of university faculty conducted in 1972 and 1980, Morgan and Newell (1982) noted a shift away from service to the field in favor of research. They concluded, "The priority placed on training, rather than on research, that was so much a part of the Kellogg years, is . . . fading" (p. 28) and noted that this could lead to strained relations with practitioners who "sometimes regard university research and theoretical knowledge as being of little or no value to practice" (p. 29). Data collected by Townsend and Wiese (1990) offer some evidence of the potential for practitioner impatience with the university's distance from day-to-day concerns. Though the administrators who responded to their survey had varying views of the practicality of doctoral studies in higher education, they tended to place a premium on university courses that emphasize finance, budgeting, and other managerial skills; courses on college teaching or the history of higher education received lower ratings of importance.

University professors, though sympathetic to the needs of practitioners, also face the demands of the academy, which focuses attention on higher education as an academic discipline. Richardson (1987) suggests that a professor's efforts to maintain credibility in the field through service to local practitioners sometimes works against the need to attain national visibility among university colleagues through research and publication. Too much attention to service, he maintains, may alienate the professor from university colleagues, while too much attention to disciplinary scholarship may alienate him or her from the practitioner. The latter danger is particularly evident, he notes, "when research findings appear inconsistent with preferred views of institutional leaders" (p. 40).

The gulf between practitioners and professors will never fully be overcome, because individuals in these two groups work in differing professional domains that make differing demands of those who pursue careers within them. But steps can be taken to foster mutually supportive relations. For example, professors can meet demands for attention to service activities that address day-to-day administrative problems by involving practitioners in research agendas, an approach advocated in Chapter Eight. Efforts can also be made to involve practitioners in the planning and development of graduate curricula. Examples include curriculum planning activities undertaken at Kent State University (Wallenfeldt and Anglin, 1990), George Mason University (Vaughan, 1989), and North Carolina State University (Academy for Community College Leadership, Advancement, Innovation, and Modeling, 1992). Attention to the importance of continuing professional education constitutes a third remedy. North Carolina State University's ACCLAIM program is an example, combining a doctoral curriculum with a set of continuing education activities for community college administrators and faculty. Noncredit programs that remain unfettered by the strictures of academic time (based on semesters or quarters) or traditions (such as comprehensive examinations and dissertations) complement degree-based education in ways that address the continually changing and idiosyncratic learning needs of college administrators. The continuing education opportunities described in Chapter Five are examples.

Conclusion

The literature on graduate preparation programs for community college education bespeaks an indistinct academic field, uncertain as to curriculum content and professorial roles. At its best, this uncertainty frees the professors to interact with students and the community college field in creative ways, unfettered by long-held norms. A professor can introduce new subjects as needed and pursue research along a variety of lines. (The diverse approaches taken by the authors of the chapters in this volume reflect this freedom.) At its worst, however, the indeterminate nature of the field diminishes the intrinsic value of the degrees awarded by graduate preparation programs. Such degrees may serve a credentialing function only, providing aspirants to leadership positions with the required doctorate without signifying what that doctorate means intellectually.

How can professors who teach in these graduate programs forge a common understanding of their work? Surely it is unrealistic to expect that total agreement will be reached about specific curriculum content and day-to-day professor-practitioner roles. But debates over these issues mask the fact that graduate preparation programs in the field of education, however diverse, have a common modus operandi: they borrow from all the social sciences, applying the insights of these disciplines to the work of schools and colleges. For example, "Studies of learning are rooted in theories from psychology and sociology; commentary on the schools is grounded in economics and political science; concepts from anthropology are used to explain teacher and student behavior" (Arthur M. Cohen, personal communication, May 1996). The application of knowledge from multiple disciplines is the core technology of professors of education. They can bring clarity to the field by studying and describing the nature of this technology, showing how access to the various disciplines enhances the administrative repertoire of community college leaders.

This technology is implied but not explicitly discussed in the literature. For example, the impact of sociology, anthropology, and political science on thinking about community college administration is evident in calls for an emphasis on democratic or feminist leadership styles. (Chapters Six and Seven illustrate this point.) Social geography emerges in the discussion in Chapter Two of a typology of community colleges, which sorts institutions into urban, suburban, and rural categories. The importance of administrative theory, which derives largely from sociology, is mentioned in Chapter Nine. The central issue facing graduate preparation programs thus lies in the questions of how interdisciplinary knowledge can be placed in the service of community college administrators and how the impact of that knowledge can be documented.

References

Academy for Community College Leadership, Advancement, Innovation, and Modeling. *The Academy for Community College Leadership, Advancement, Innovation, and Modeling.* Raleigh: North Carolina State University, 1992. (ED 340 438)

Alfred, R. L. *Community College.* Washington, D.C.: Association for the Study of Higher Education, 1986. (ED 272 119)

Dressel, P. L., and Mayhew, L. B. *Higher Education as a Field of Study: The Emergence of a Profession.* San Francisco: Jossey-Bass, 1974.

Fryer, T. W., Jr. "Developing Leaders Through Graduate Education." In R. L. Alfred, P. A. Elsner, R. J. LeCroy, and N. Armes (eds.), *Emerging Roles for Community College Leaders.* New Directions for Community Colleges, no. 46. San Francisco: Jossey-Bass, 1984.

Goodchild, L. F. "Higher Education as a Field of Study: Its Origins, Programs, and Purposes, 1893–1960." In J. D. Fife and L. F. Goodchild (eds.), *Administration as a Profession.* New Directions for Higher Education, no. 76. San Francisco: Jossey-Bass, 1991.

Keim, M. C. "Graduate Preparation Programs in Community College Education." *Community College Review,* 1994, 22 (1), 53–61.

Lumsden, D. B. "Opportunities in Community College Education." *Community College Review,* 1981, 9 (3), 37–49.

Lumsden, D. B., and Stewart, G. B. "American Colleges and Universities Offering Course Work on Two-Year Institutions: Results of a National Study." *Community College Review,* 1992a, 19 (4), 34–46.

Lumsden, D. B., and Stewart, G. B. *Graduate-Level Courses on Two-Year Institutions: Directory.* Washington, D.C.: American Association of Community and Junior Colleges, 1992b. (ED 363 369)

Miller, M. T., and Nelson, G. M. *Graduate Programs in the Study of Higher Education: Selected Syllabi.* Lincoln: Department of Educational Administration, University of Nebraska, 1993. (ED 363 238)

Morgan, D. A., and Newell, L. J. "Professors of Community College Education: Changes in Theoretical and Professional Orientations." *Community/Junior College Quarterly of Research and Practice,* 1982, 7 (1), 15–29.

Rahaim, C. *Field-Based Doctoral Program for Community College Personnel: The First Five Years.* Amherst: School of Education, University of Massachusetts, 1983. (ED 279 352)

Ratcliff, J. L. *The Comprehensive Community College: Study Guide.* Ames: College of Education, Iowa State University, 1986. (ED 269 092)

Richardson, R. C., Jr. "A Question of Quality: University Programs for Community College Leaders." *Community, Technical, and Junior College Journal,* 1987, 57 (4), 39–41.

Townsend, B. K., and Wiese, M. "Value of the Higher Education Doctorate For Community College Administrators." *Community/Junior College Quarterly of Research and Practice,* 1990, 14 (4), 337–347.

Vaughan, G. B. *Doctorate of Arts in Community College Education.* Fairfax, Va.: George Mason University, 1989. (ED 316 116)

Wallenfeldt, E. C., and Anglin, L. W. *Institutional Partnership: An Evolving Case Study.* Kent, Ohio: Graduate School of Education, Kent State University, 1990. (ED 326 279)

JAMES C. PALMER *is associate professor of educational administration and foundations at Illinois State University, Normal, Illinois.*

STEPHEN G. KATSINAS *is associate professor of higher education at the University of Toledo, Toledo, Ohio.*

Index

Ordering Information

New Directions for Community Colleges is a series of paperback books that provides expert assistance to help community colleges meet the challenges of their distinctive and expanding educational mission. Books in the series are published quarterly in Spring, Summer, Fall, and Winter and are available for purchase by subscription and individually.

Subscriptions cost $53.00 for individuals (a savings of 34 percent over single-copy prices) and $89.00 for institutions, agencies, and libraries. Please do not send institutional checks for personal subscriptions. Standing orders are accepted. (For subscriptions outside of North America, add $7.00 for shipping via surface mail or $25.00 for air mail. Orders *must be prepaid* in U.S. dollars by check drawn on a U.S. bank or charged to VISA, MasterCard, or American Express.)

Single copies cost $20.00 plus shipping (see below) when payment accompanies order. California, New Jersey, New York, and Washington, D.C. residents please include appropriate sales tax. Canadian residents add GST and any local taxes. Billed orders will be charged shipping and handling. No billed shipments to post office boxes. (Orders from outside North America *must be prepaid* in U.S. dollars by check drawn on a U.S. bank or charged to VISA, MasterCard, or American Express.)

Shipping (Single Copies Only): $10.00 and under, add $2.50; to $20.00, add $3.50; to $50.00, add $4.50; to $75.00, add $5.50; to $100.00, add $6.50; to $150.00, add $7.50; over $150.00, add $8.50.

Discounts for quantity orders are available. Please write to the address below for information.

All orders must include either the name of an individual or an official purchase order number. Please submit your order as follows:
Subscriptions: specify series and year subscription is to begin
Single copies: include individual title code (such as CC82)

Mail all orders to:
Jossey-Bass Publishers
350 Sansome Street
San Francisco, California 94104-1342

For subscription sales outside of the United States, contact any international subscription agency or Jossey-Bass directly.